BARKA

BARRA

Episodes from an Island's History

KEITH BRANIGAN

AMBERLEY

For Nancy and Ian Roderick MacNeil[†]of Barra

First published 2012

Amberley Publishing
The Hill, Stroud
Gloucestershire, GL5 4EP

www.amberley-books.com

British Library Cataloguing in Publication Data.
A catalogue record for this book is available from the British Library.

ISBN 978 1 84868 871 1

Typeset in 10pt on 12pt Sabon.
Typesetting and Origination by Amberley Publishing.
Printed in the UK.

CONTENTS

Keith Branigan has carried out archaeological and historical research on Barra for over twenty years and written six previous books reporting his discoveries. His researches into Barra's past have taken him to Nova Scotia, Cape Breton and Prince Edward Island as well as to Italy. With colleagues from Sheffield University, he has discovered and recorded almost 2,000 archaeological sites on the Barra islands and excavated fifty of them. He is currently Professor Emeritus of Archaeology & Prehistory at the University of Sheffield.

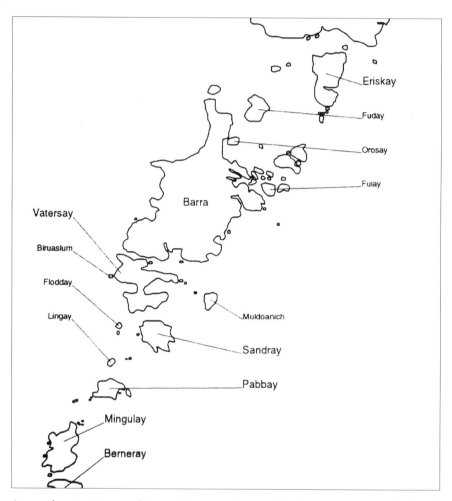

Eriskay

Fuday

Orosay

Fuiay

Barra

Vatersay

Biruaslum

Flodday

Lingay

Muldoanich

Sandray

Pabbay

Mingulay

Berneray

A map showing Barra and its neighbouring islands, all of which pertained to Macneil of Barra in the seventeenth century.

Introduction

I was delighted when Amberley asked me if I would write another book about Barra after I had completed my biography of General Roderick Macneil (*The Last of the Clan*, Amberley 2010). Apart from three volumes of detailed archaeological reports, my previous books on Barra include a guide to its sites and monuments (*Ancient Barra*, Comhairle nan Eilean Siar 2007) and the book I co-authored with Patrick Foster – *Barra and the Bishop's Isles* (Tempus 2002). That book was essentially an overview of the prehistory and archaeology of the islands focusing on material remains and culture. Patrick and I were both archaeologists by training and career and the twelve-year project we began on Barra in 1988 was primarily an archaeological project. Inevitably much of the archaeology we were involved with belonged to the historical period, and I became increasingly drawn into researching the history of the islands as well as their archaeology. This interest was partly reflected in the opening and concluding chapters of *From Clan to Clearance* (Oxbow 2005), which were historical rather than archaeological, and in my biography of the General. Amberley's invitation to write another book was welcome because it provided me with an opportunity to look in more detail at some of the islands' fascinating historical episodes while also providing visitors to the islands with an overview of the islands' history.

Although the title of the book includes only the name of Barra the scope of the book includes all those islands which were at one time or another included in the territory pertaining to the Macneil of Barra. The southernmost of the islands is Berneray, only 3 km at its greatest extent, steeply pitched from south to north with 180-metre-high vertical cliffs forming its southern edge. Here stands the iconic Barra Head lighthouse, built inside an Iron Age fortification. Approaching the island from Barra on a nice day it appears like a vivid green wedge, but in winter its east–west orientation leaves it wide open to the fierce Atlantic gales. Despite its remote location and exposure to wild weather, in the mid-nineteenth century it was home to about thirty people as well as the lighthouse crew.

North of Berneray is the island of Mingulay best known around the world for its haunting 'Mingulay Boat Song', conjuring up images of its brave fishermen pitting their skills against wind and weather in the Minches, but actually written by a Glaswegian almost thirty years after the last families abandoned the island. But Mingulay is, nevertheless, a wonderful island, with four hills which from the east appear to be great waves sweeping across the sea, frozen in time. Like Berneray its western aspect is dominated by massive cliffs which are the home to thousands of seabirds. Its abandoned village, which once housed about 150 people, is fronted by a sandy bay, but landing a boat on the island was always difficult and is one of the reasons it was eventually abandoned.

Above Mingulay lies the small island of Pabbay, about 2 km long and a little less wide. It has an attractive sandy bay on its east side, behind which lies the only small area of arable land on the island and the ancient cemetery mound and a Bronze Age village. The island was never occupied in historical times by more than a couple of dozen people and in the late nineteenth century was famed locally for the whisky which was illicitly produced there. Although it has cliffs up to 120 metres high they are not extensive or awesome like those of Berneray and Mingulay, and the rest of the island lacks the beauty to be found in the islands to the north of it. In places, as Ben Buxton has observed, 'it is a rather sinister place'.

Sandray, about 4 km north of Pabbay, is roughly circular and about 3 km across. It is a little like a miniature version of Barra in that it has a high rocky centre and areas of machair and low pastures around its coastal fringe. On the east side the drifting sand creates huge dunes, so that settlement has tended to be focused on the west side, and particularly at the preferred site of Sheader at its north-western tip. In the eighteenth century over three dozen people lived on the island but for much of the nineteenth century it was rented out for grazing and occupied only by shepherds. Sandray has the feel of a friendly place to live, and seen on a sunny summer morning with the remains of the Iron Age tower perched on a rocky crag overlooking Loch na Cuilce it can seem quite magical.

Close to the north shore of Sandray is the south coast of Vatersay, the southernmost of the occupied islands. It is an unusual island being two unequal halves of quite different character joined together only by a sandy isthmus less than 400 metres wide. South Vatersay is a gentle landscape with rolling green pastures covered with flowers including wonderful orchids, rising to high points of only 80 metres at its eastern and western extremities. The isthmus is covered with machair and has two superb sweeping beaches. North Vatersay is dominated by Heishival Mhor which rises to 190 metres and has a rugged coastline. At its western end it is separated by a sea dyke from the small island of Biruaslam. Around Caolis and Traigh Varlish there is some pasture and machair, and the eastern peninsula of Uidh has a series of small but attractive bays and beaches. Vatersay's population has varied much over time, with eighty to a hundred people living there in the late seventeenth century, reduced to twenty to thirty when it was let out to farmers from the mid-nineteenth century. After it was turned into crofts at the beginning of the twentieth century the population rocketed to almost 300, but gradually it diminished again until *c.* 1985 it was down to about sixty. The building of the causeway to Barra in 1990 has fortunately reversed the trend.

Barra is of course the focus of this group of islands being by far the biggest, though still a small island. It is roughly 8 km square, with projecting peninsulas at the south-west (Tangaval), north-east (Bruernish) and north (Eoligarry). These peninsulas are very different from each other, with a very mountainous Tangaval reaching well over 300 metres, a lower but bleak and boggy Bruernish, and a green machair-covered Eoligarry dominated by Ben Eoligarry at 100 metres. Eoligarry is famous for its cockle beach, a source of sustenance in times of famine throughout the ages, and the site of Barra's tidal airport. The central mass of Barra is dominated by high steep hills – Heaval at 380 metres, Hartaval at 350 metres, Ben Cliat and Ben Erival at 200 metres. On the east side of the island the hill slopes run right down to the sea except for a small valley around Brevig, but the west coast has important areas of machair and low pasture, and some fine beaches. At the southern end of the island is Castlebay in the waters of which sits of course the 'Castle in the Sea' – Kisimul Castle, ancestral home of the Macneils of Barra. The island's population for most of the nineteenth century remained between 1,500 and 2,000, despite emigration, and peaked in 1901 at 2,400. A decline through the twentieth century was reversed in the last decades and the island currently has about 1,300 people.

The last of the islands is Eriskay, only 4.5 km in length with a high point towards the north end of 185 metres. It is a somewhat barren island but has achieved fame for its 'Eriskay Love Lilt', the fact that Bonnie Prince Charlie landed here to begin the 1745 Jacobite rebellion, and for the shipwreck of SS *Politician* in 1941. The ship carried in its hold over 250,000 bottles of whisky, to which the local people took a fancy. The story was immortalised by Sir Compton Mackenzie in his book *Whisky Galore*. The island passed out of Macneil possession in 1758, and was bought by Gordon of Cluny in 1838.

All of these islands, from Berneray to Eriskay, feature at some point in this book though inevitably Barra gets the lion's share of attention. The chapters are arranged in chronological order and although they focus on a series of episodes in the islands' history I have tried to link them together in such a way that they also give a reasonably continuous overview of the whole period from *c.* 3500 BC to the early twentieth century. The snapshots of the islands' history vary considerably in their 'exposure' time. The first two chapters each cover more than a millennium, the next three several centuries, and chapters six to eight about a century each. Most of the remaining chapters are concerned with periods of ten to fifty years, except for chapter eleven which focuses on the events of just two months in 1853. Similarly the 'lens' through which each 'snapshot' is taken changes from the 'wide angle' used to look at entire, anonymous communities and general processes in prehistory, to the 'close-up' homing in on individuals and specific events as we move closer to our own time.

As I mentioned earlier, the book is aimed particularly at the visitor to Barra who wants to know more about the history of these beautiful islands. For that reason I have made more use in this book of the colourful oral traditions kept alive both by the islanders themselves and by the Clan Macneil. The backbone of the book, however, remains the evidence provided by archaeology and historical documents. For those who want to delve deeper into some of these episodes I also provide a short list of suggestions for further reading.

Pioneers – The First Settlers

The history of Barra must begin, I suppose, around 3,000 million years BC, when the hard and ugly gneiss rock of which the island is made was forming. But human occupation of course began very much more recently. It was only when the great ice sheets melted around 10,000 BC, that the Western Isles became accessible to, and inhabitable by, human populations. As the ice finally retreated northwards, the trough between what we now call the Scottish mainland and the Outer Hebrides was quickly inundated and the Long Island from Lewis to Berneray was formed. The retreating ice left behind a landscape of smoothed hills, ice-moulded hillocks and water-filled basins. Light woodland developed rapidly as the climate warmed. Pollen recovered from below the waters of Lochan na Cartach on the east side of Barra and pollen recovered from Borve headland on the west side of the island comes almost entirely from birch and hazel woodland. In time larger species such as oak and elm took root, but always in much smaller numbers.

Just when the first humans set foot on Barra is still uncertain, though it seems unlikely it was much after 8000 BC, by which time they were already living on Rhum and Skye. But archaeologists have so far failed to find any clear traces of these 'Mesolithic' hunters anywhere in the Western Isles. The flimsy traces of their shelters may have been submerged by blanket peat, by sand, and by the sea which has covered over a mile of former land off the west coast of Barra. This inundated landscape was covered with woodland and at low tide it is still possible to see the remains of Mesolithic trees on the edge of Borve headland.

The earliest settlers yet known on Barra arrived there around 4000 BC, and we know three of the places where they settled. One was on the tiny island of Biruaslum off the west coast of Vatersay, another was by the side of Loch Obe at Balnabodach, and the third was at Allt Easdal on the south coast of Barra. Although these people still hunted, fished and gathered wild foods, they were also farmers and they made pottery, so we label them as 'Neolithic'.

A map showing some of the places mentioned in the text.

These pioneer settlers faced problems which were largely unknown to their contemporaries on the mainland. The soil over most of the island was thin, and the underlying rock was hard and awkward to use for building. Peat had begun to develop on some of the higher and wetter ground. There had never been much heavy woodland, and even the hazel and birch were beginning to decline by this time, so wood both for building and fuel was a diminishing commodity. Furthermore, the island had no mineral resources and even flint for small tools and implements could only be found as small pebbles gathered from the beaches. The climate was relatively mild, but high winds made it difficult to grow crops. The people who settled at Allt Easdal would have to learn to adapt to these conditions if they were to survive. Carbon dates recovered from the lower and highest occupation levels show that they learned to adapt so well that they stayed on this single small site generation after generation, for over a thousand years!

Why they chose this spot in the first place is something of a mystery. It has been described as 'sheltered' but on this rather bleak and bare southern coastline, that is a relative term. Certainly, when we first discovered the site in March 1989 and crouched low behind the biggest rock we could find to avoid being peppered with horizontal hail driving in from the Atlantic, sheltered was not a description that first came to mind. Nor are the lower slopes of Ben Tangaval endowed with deep rich soils for growing crops, or covered with lush grass to raise stock. The only features going for the site at Allt Easdal are the bubbling freshwater stream that runs down the shallow valley, and the immediate proximity of the Sound of Vatersay with its possibilities for catching seafood and seabirds.

Whatever their reasons, however, the first settlers had almost certainly spent some time in the area before they put down permanent roots at Allt Easdal, and equally, when they took the decision to settle down here, they clearly intended to stay for some time. We can say that because we found that the flat platform on which they built they homes was a substantial artificial construction. The settlers had built a rough revetment of large boulders, and then collected and carried to the site thousands of smaller rocks and stones and dumped them behind the revetment to level up the slope and produce a flat area about 12 metres square. They then spread soil over the stone rubble

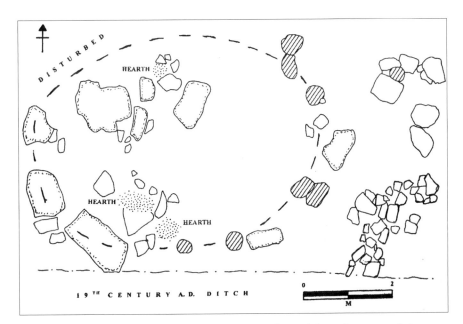

Remains of a timber-framed hut of *c.* 3500 BC at Allt Easdal. At the west end the posts may have stood on the rock 'pads', and within the oval there were small domestic hearths.

at the front of the platform to make it a comfortable surface on which to live. Only people who knew they wanted to stay here for many years to come would have gone to all this trouble.

The remains left behind by these pioneer settlers were partly destroyed when a blackhouse was built on the invitingly flat and solid space at the front of the platform in the late eighteenth century. This area was sliced off almost down to the base of the prehistoric occupation. Fortunately, although the crofters removed stone slabs from the rear area to help build their house, the accumulated occupation deposits were here left mostly undisturbed. Careful excavation of these revealed something of the character of the settlement occupied by the first arrivals.

The settlers had polished stone axes capable of felling trees, and initially they seem to have preferred to build in timber. An arc of post holes and post pads (flat slabs of stone and bare rock on which posts could be stood) delineated an oval area about 6 metres by 4 metres. Within this area were two adjacent hearth areas. The upright timber posts would have supported a thatched roof, and possibly panels of wattle which when daubed with clay would have provided a wind- and rain-proof wall. But it is possible that the oval enclosing wall was built of turf, and stood further out beyond the timber roof supports, so that the hut might have measured say 8 metres by 6 metres, and provided twice as much floor space. Apart from the hearths inside the house, there were more hearths and cooking hollows in the area immediately

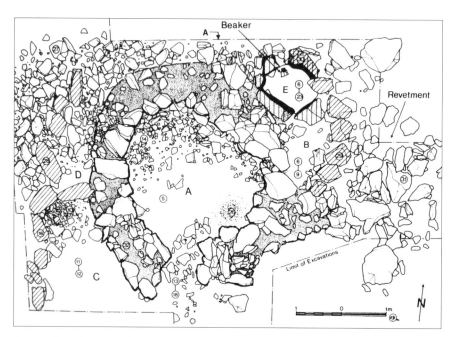

A stone-based circular hut at Allt Easdal dated *c.* 2300 BC, with a hearth just to one side of the door and a stone-built storage box on its back wall.

outside, and pottery and flint tools and debris were spread across the platform.

Two of the hut's timber posts were replaced at some time so the hut was probably occupied for some decades, but eventually it was demolished. It was not replaced by another building on the same spot, so that the settlers moved to live either on the front of the platform (where the blackhouse would be built nearly 6,000 years later) or somewhere else in the vicinity. The new house may well have been built mainly of stone since wood for a timber-framed house was becoming increasingly scarce. The type is demonstrated by a later Neolithic house built further up the hill slope, about 2500 BC, which had a thick wall lined on both faces with stone and a packed earth core, and was about 4.5 metres in diameter. The rear of the platform at Allt Easdal was now given over to a variety of activities which tell us something about the lives of these Neolithic pioneers. The most fundamental activity for any human group is the acquisition, preparation and consumption of food and this is evidenced by various materials recovered from the platform. Charred cereal grains confirm that the first settlers brought seed grain with them and managed to grow barley somewhere close by. Primitive millstones and pebble rubbers were probably used to grind the grain into flour, but it may also have been used to make a beer. Meat was acquired mainly from sheep but cattle and a few pigs were kept. Shellfish, seals, and seabirds added variety to the diet, and fish were caught in nets with floats made from Icelandic pumice found on the beaches. These foods were cooked not only in small hollows but in carefully built stone-lined hearths.

Sheep also provided wool and skins and cattle supplied milk and leather. Small flint tools made to scrape skins clean, and to cut them and pierce them for sewing together, were found in quantity among the settlement debris. What is amazing about the tool kits produced at Allt Easdal is their miniature size. With mostly only small sea-worn flint pebbles as raw material, their makers had excelled themselves in producing scaled-down versions of the tools made

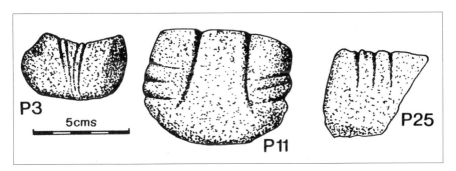

Pieces of pumice used as floats for fishing nets from Neolithic Allt Easdal. The pumice was picked up from the beaches, and came from Iceland originally.

One of two rectangular stone-lined hearths found in the Neolithic settlement at Allt Easdal.

and used on the mainland. Thumbnail scrapers (so named after their shape), awls or borers, and small knife blades provided the skin and leather workers with the tools they needed to produce clothes, bags, hats and shoes. The absence of spindle whorls and loom-weights might suggest that in fact leather and skin clothing was *de rigueur* for the pioneers.

These tools were made at the settlement site, on the rear platform, which seems to have become the focus of craft activities. At one end of the platform an area of about 15 metres square was covered with a rough paving of irregular blocks of gneiss, which we (rather grandly) labelled 'the patio'. Its purpose is uncertain; we certainly don't think it was used for sunbathing or afternoon tea parties. But the effort put into constructing it suggests that it had a useful part to play in the activities on the platform. We wonder if it was used to lay skins out to dry and then to clean. On the west side it was flanked by an arc of drystone wall foundation, which could have been completed with either a stone or turf superstructure. It may have served to keep anyone working on the patio free from smoke and burning cinders when the wind was blowing from the west.

The west end of the patio certainly had a concentration of hearths and fireplaces, many of which were used for domestic cooking, but others appear to have been used for a different purpose. These were not shallow hollows filled with burnt debris, but slight mounds of very brightly burnt soil with a rather fibrous texture. One of these was more prominent than the others and when it was excavated it was found to contain the collapsed sherds of a single large deep bowl. This appears to have been the remains of a turf 'clamp' (a primitive kiln of piled-up turf) in which the pot was being fired. The similar mounds of burnt fibrous soil nearby were presumably all that survived from other, more successful firings from which the pots had been removed. So some of the pottery used at the settlement appears to have been made on the spot.

Altogether the remains of between 700 and 1,000 pottery vessels were recovered from the rear of the platform. The vessels fell into three main groups. Big and rather deep, somewhat baggy jars and bowls were probably used for both storage and cooking. Smaller, shallow bowls were more suitable for serving up individual portions of food, and may also have been used in the earlier years of the settlement's existence to serve drinks. By the time the settlement was abandoned, however, distinctive tall beakers were being used for this purpose. More than the half the pots, mostly the cooking and storage jars, were left undecorated by their makers, but the other vessels showed a remarkably wide range of decorative techniques and motifs.

Pottery decoration at this time consisted of incising or impressing a design into the pot's surface before it was fired; there was no painted decoration. Since the pots were all fired to a dark- or reddish-brown colour, they were a rather drab lot to have about the house, so decoration made them more attractive and interesting for those who used them. Incised lines made with

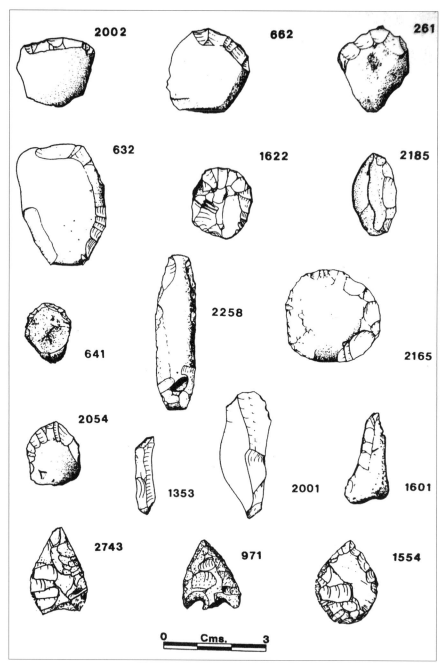

Examples of the miniature stone tools made from pebble flints found on the beaches. They include thumbnail scrapers (for cleaning skins), blades, points or awls, and arrowheads.

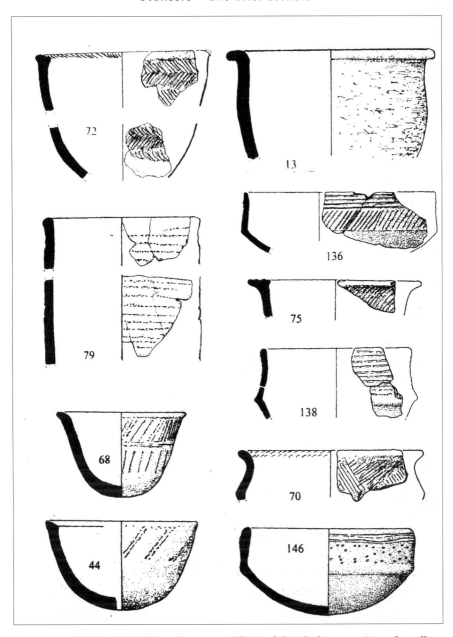

Pottery used in the Neolithic settlement at Allt Easdal including a variety of small bowls and larger, deeper storage vessels.

a sharp-edged flint blade were commonly arranged in rows of oblique lines set in alternating directions to produce a herringbone pattern. More rarely blocks of horizontal lines were separated by blocks of vertical ones. A distinctive type of bowl with an upright side and shallow rounded base was regularly decorated on the upper part with three or four parallel horizontal lines above a close-set series of oblique lines which ran around the entire pot. Some beakers were decorated with incised lines too, but most had impressed decoration. Continuous cord impressions, made by winding a cord round and round the pot while the clay was soft, was a popular pattern, but impressions were also made with the teeth of bone combs and the edge of seashells. Whether the decoration had any symbolic meaning or signified ownership or identity, or whether it was produced purely for pleasure and interest, is unknown.

Nevertheless the pottery tells us not only about the domestic life of the pioneers at Allt Easdal, but also about their contacts with the world beyond Barra. The shallow bowls with upright sides, for example, are known as Unstan Ware and are found throughout the Western Isles and in Orkney and Shetland. A bowl of similar shape, but decorated with a series of dots impressed with a bone point, is a close relation of a similar bowl found at Isbister in Orkney. The beaker vessels on the other hand are part of a family

Neolithic sherds with a wide variety of decorative methods including incision, grooving and shell and bone impressions.

found over much of Western Europe and have particularly close similarities to examples from the mainland of Scotland. The stone artefacts recovered from the site confirm these links, with examples made of Rhum bloodstone, Arran and Eigg pitchstone, and Antrim porcellanite. So though it is easy to think of Barra as remote and somewhat isolated towards the bottom of the Long Island, even in these early days of human occupation the sea acted as much as a corridor as it did a barrier for contact with the islands to the north, the inner islands and the mainland to the east, and Ireland to the south.

These contacts are strongly reflected in the funerary architecture, and possibly therefore in the funerary customs and beliefs, of the Neolithic population of Barra. By 3000 BC they were building big stone cairns with a burial chamber made of large slabs at their centre, approached by a stone-lined passage. This type of tomb is found in other parts of the Western Isles and in western Scotland. The nearest example to Allt Easdal is a kilometre away, in Cornaig Bay on the north coast of Vatersay. The cairn is about 12 metres wide but has been robbed of most of its stone so we do not know how high it stood. But most of the large stones lining the entrance passage and the

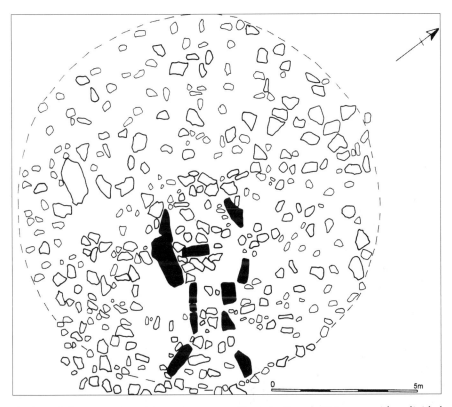

A plan of the unexcavated passage grave at Cornaig Bay on Vatersay, with a divided burial chamber and passage of upright megaliths, and the remains of the covering cairn of stones.

chamber are still in place. It has never been excavated though it may well have been looted in much earlier times. The Cornaig Bay cairn is dwarfed, however, by another 'passage grave' at Dun Bharpa, about 5 km (as the crow flies) northeast of Allt Easdal. This cairn is about 30 metres across and still stands about 5 metres high. The huge capping slab of its burial chamber is visible, and some of the entrance passage slabs. Most interesting of all are the upright stone slabs set into the perimeter of the cairn. Fifteen of them survive, the tallest about 4 metres high. They do not make a complete ring, and being set into the edge of the cairn they may well have been added to the monument one at a time. In that case it is tempting to think that each stone represents a single burial, and therefore also represents a particular, individual ancestor. Elsewhere on Barra a few 'standing stones' are found either standing alone or in pairs, and they too are thought to belong to this era and represent stones erected as memorials to ancestors.

The passage graves involved a massive amount of effort on the part of the local population. The cairn at Dun Bharpa, as it survives, comprises well over 100 cubic metres of stone which had to be collected and carted here from the areas around. This could have been done over a long period of time by a small number of people, but dragging the huge covering slab to the site and hauling it into place at the top of the cairn would have needed many hands and some skill and experience. The slabs for the chamber and passage, and the monoliths set up around the perimeter, would also have required a lot of manpower to bring them to the cairn and manoeuvre them into position. Many families must have come together to build Dun Bharpa, and probably therefore to participate in the funerary ceremonies performed there. But whether everyone was entitled to be buried there, or whether it was restricted to certain families or certain individuals, is unknown.

The great third millennium BC passage grave of Dun Bharpa with its massive cairn and incomplete ring of standing stones.

It seems likely that some inhabitants of Allt Easdal were buried nearer to hand. About 400 metres east of the settlement a much smaller tomb was erected, with a passage and burial chamber surrounded by a heel-shaped cairn with a flat facade. Its nearest relations are found in Ireland. Another heel-shaped cairn was found further north at Greian, but that example has a much broader facade and is more like tombs found in Shetland. These small heel-shaped tombs were probably built some centuries after the big passage graves, and they may reflect a transition to funerary monuments and ceremonies focused more on the individual family than the larger community. The nearest tomb of all to Allt Easdal, probably not built until around 2000 BC, points to the same conclusion. Perched on a ledge about 135 metres above the settlement, this tomb was a low cairn surrounded by a roughly built wall, inside of which stone blocks had been laid to form a very uneven 'pavement'. It had an in-turned entrance on the south-facing side, with a large blocking stone, and inside was a cist built of slabs set upright. Two flat slabs nearby were probably the original covering stones of the cist. We presume a burial was originally placed in the cist, but the acidic soil would long ago have disposed of any skeletal remains, and excavation yielded nothing but a single piece of flint. The interest of this tomb is that it seems to represent a step in the transition from the passage grave tradition of burial preserving an in-turned entrance and blocking slab, to the kerbed cairns which became popular in this area in the second millennium BC.

It is a pity that the soils in the area around Allt Easdal did not allow the preservation of any skeletal material in either the heeled or the paved cairn. After all, when we are looking at a 'snapshot' of these Neolithic pioneers what we most want to see are the people themselves. What were they like? Fortunately the remains of people living at the same time in similar conditions in the northern islands are better preserved and from them we can learn something about the physical appearance and condition of the pioneers. They were of medium build, men around 165–175 cm tall, women about 10 cm shorter. Their relatively poor diet and the hard work they put into farming, fishing, and tomb building meant they were probably lean but muscular. Not surprisingly many of them suffered from degenerative spine diseases and arthritis was a common complaint. On the other hand their diet ensured that their teeth were generally in good condition. Nevertheless life was clearly hard and took its toll at an early age. Few men lived beyond forty and women beyond their early thirties; child mortality was high.

Yet as a population rather than as individuals we have seen that these people clung tenaciously to life. They adapted quickly to the environmental constraints of the Western Isles, developed considerable skills in stone working and pottery production, and utilised to the full the limited food and raw material resources available to them. By dint of hard work, skill, and sheer persistence they carved out a viable lifestyle. Their most amazing achievement, however, was to develop such a strong sense of identity, place and belonging that they remained living at Allt Easdal for over a thousand years!

2

Mourners – Death and the Dead in the Bronze Age

The fact that we know so much about how the pioneer settlers of Barra lived is, frankly, down to exceptional good luck. Their settlement site at Allt Easdal was found only because we were excavating the overlying blackhouse, and the same was true of the Neolithic remains discovered at Balnabodach. Only the 'Beaker' hut at Allt Easdal was identified in survey, and even there we had no certainty about its date until we excavated it. Otherwise, our idea of Neolithic Barra would have been restricted to the megalithic tombs like Dun Bharpa, Balnacraig, and Cornaig Bay. When we come to the Bronze Age we have not been so fortunate, and apart from some interesting but rather simple structural features found beneath an early Iron Age hut in the Borve valley we have no excavated Bronze Age settlement remains at all. There are about a dozen round huts on Barra and Vatersay which for various reasons we think are probably of Bronze Age date, but we have no firm proof of this. As a result, our view of the Bronze Age landscape of the islands is at present dominated by monuments associated with burying and commemorating the dead. If we were to judge them purely on the basis of the visible remains they have left behind we could easily conclude that the people of Bronze Age Barra were a gloomy lot who spent their time and energy mourning dead friends and relatives.

One aspect of this behaviour which seems to be carried over from the later Neolithic is the use of standing stones, either set up individually or in rings, as representatives or memorials of ancestors. We have already noted the ring of monoliths set up around the edge of the Dun Bharpa chambered tomb, where a connection between standing stones and the dead is quite explicit. At the end of the third millennium BC we see the possible incorporation of that relationship into the newly emerging pattern of smaller burial cairns without chambers like the 'paved' one above Allt Easdal. This tomb and a similar but unexcavated example near Cleat both have a monolith associated with them. At about this time stone rings, composed of between ten and thirty upright stones, were constructed at several sites on Barra with others on Vatersay and Mingulay. None are very spectacular to our eyes, because Barra and the southern isles are very short of long, narrow stones which make impressive monoliths. But they nevertheless required a considerable amount of time and energy to move and erect the stones. Like the more impressive stone circles found elsewhere in Britain there is little doubt that they were used for communal and probably seasonal rituals. Recently archaeologists have begun to think that those rituals were in some way involved with the ancestors.

Elsewhere individual monoliths were set up as 'standing stones', believed to represent or commemorate ancestors. The best-preserved example still standing on Barra overlooks Brevig and stands 3.2 metres tall. Broken fragments of a second stone, which was once of a similar height, lie nearby. A second pair of stones stood on Borve headland, the taller at least 2.9 metres high originally but both now reduced and one almost totally destroyed. Most of the standing stones have long since fallen (or been deliberately pushed over) and by far the most impressive of all these is that lying in the Pass of the Mouth which connects the east and west coasts of Barra. When we cleared off the encroaching peat bog, the stone was found to be over 6 metres long.

Standing stones and stone rings were probably constructed from the late Neolithic through into the earlier Bronze Age and suggest some continuity in beliefs and practices to do with the ancestors at this time. A third type of monument – the so-called 'giant cists' – may also reflect a combination of

Remains of a 'giant cist' covered by peat and heather high on an exposed ridge above Bretadale on the south-west coast of Barra.

continuity and change in the funerary practices of this time. The 'giant cists' are not only unique to Barra; they have been found only on one hillside even there. When one of our archaeological survey teams came back one day and said they had found four or five megalithic tombs overlooking the bleak and remote valley of Bretadale we were intrigued but decidedly sceptical. A long and tiring climb up the steep hillside and through the soggy peat bogs next day brought us to an overgrown megalithic structure about 9 metres long and approaching 3 metres wide at its broadest end. It definitely looked interesting so we set about searching for the other three or four structures mentioned by the survey team. By the end of the day we had discovered eight of them, some better preserved than others, ranging between 7 metres and 9 metres long. They all appeared to be wedge-shaped, have one end broader than the other, and all had their biggest stones, set upright, around the broad end. They certainly looked like close relations of the passages and burial chambers of many of the passage graves of north Britain. But there were two striking differences. None of the structures revealed any trace of ever having had covering slabs, and none of them showed the slightest sign of being covered by a cairn. We wondered what they were and when they were built and used.

To try and get more information to answer those questions we undertook the excavation of one of the 'cists'. Once cleared, we could see that the structure was indeed wedge-shaped, being 2.8 metres wide at the west end and 2.2 metres at the east. The biggest stone, a monster over 1 metre square, stood bang in the middle of the west wall, flanked on either side by further stones almost as tall. The stones were found to get smaller as one moved eastwards, and the east 'wall' itself was composed of small blocks which one could step over or easily move aside. In essence, we seemed to have a structure which was entered from the east end and which ended in a broad 'chamber' enclosed by

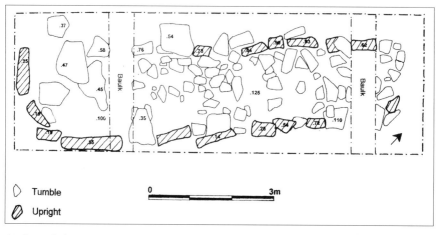

A plan of the excavated 'giant cist' at Bretadale; note its wedge shape and the big stones at its west end.

tall stones at the west end. The fact that all eight of the 'cists' we had found appeared to share these features suggested that their shape and the use of large megaliths at the broad end were regarded as important aspects of these structures.

By clearing the entire inside of the excavated example we were able to understand how it had been erected. The bedrock had been completely cleared of overlying soil and the monoliths and blocks which made up the cist's walls had then been manoeuvred into position on the bare rock. This was important because it meant that the peat inside the structure had accumulated after it was built, and presumably after it went out of use. In the absence of any dateable artefacts we had to rely on C^{14} dating of the peat to tell us how old the cist was. Two C^{14} dates provided brackets of *c.* 1940–1460 BC. So the cist probably went out of use sometime in the early second millenium BC.

Given the soil conditions we did not expect to find any skeletal remains in the structure even if it had originally held them, but burials in megalithic tombs were usually accompanied by small quantities of pottery, flint implements and other items. Despite careful excavation of the cist we found not a single piece of pottery or flint inside it. Along with the lack of evidence for covering slabs or a cairn, this meant it was very unlikely that the structure had been used as a tomb. But in that case what had they been used for? The absence of pottery and flint meant that it was equally unlikely that the structures had been used for living in even on a seasonal basis. Their exposed location made the 'cists' unsuitable places for storage, shelter, or stock pens, nor would such usage explain why they had all been built in such a specific form.

The structures were clearly 'special' in some way, built to a distinctive plan with echoes of megalithic tombs, and uniquely found grouped together on just one remote hillside. The only explanation we could think of, which fitted all the known facts, was that they had been used as mortuary enclosures where bodies were exposed until they had been reduced to skeletal remains, which may then have been removed for burial elsewhere. Such enclosures, mostly long and narrow, are known from other parts of Britain at this time, in other regions often built of timber and/or turf. If our interpretation is correct it still leaves two important questions unanswered. First, were the eight cists above Bretadale all built and used at one time, or one after the other? Without taking C^{14} samples from all of them it is impossible to say, but we suspect they were all in use at more or less the same time and that this remote exposed ridge had been selected as the one place on Barra where bodies would be exposed in this way. In that case, each cist or enclosure might have been used by an extended kin-group or a specific community. The second unanswered question is, if bones were removed for burial elsewhere, where were those permanent tombs to be found? One possibility is the passage graves, whose period of usage may have just about overlapped with the period of the enclosures. Another

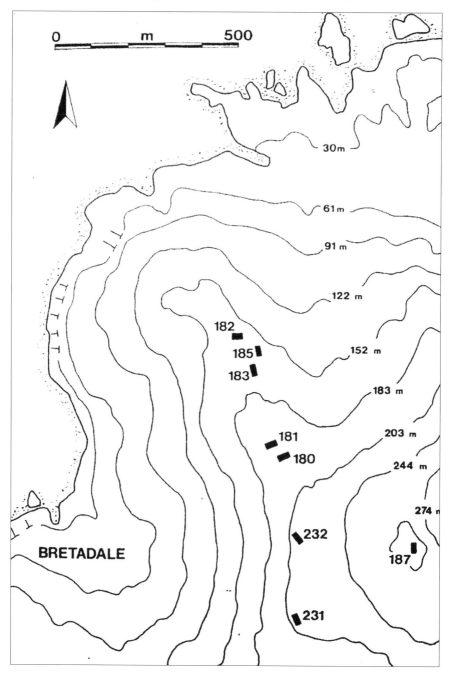

A map showing the location of the unique 'giant cists' – found only on this one hillside on Barra.

The kerbstones of a kerbed cairn showing through the turf, with a flat 'berm' inside the kerb and a low cairn at the centre.

destination for the bones might be the smaller circular cairns that are found on the islands from the earlier Bronze Age onwards.

Altogether we recorded over ninety circular cairns of probably Bronze Age date on Barra and the southern isles. Most (thirty-eight) were found on Vatersay, and Mingulay (twenty-two), while by far the largest island, Barra, yielded only fourteen. These cairns can be divided into two types. 'Kerbed cairns' have a circle of stone blocks laid to form a flat-topped kerb around their periphery. Inside the kerb there is a flat 'berm' before the cairn rises up to cover the central area. 'Bordered cairns' are also surrounded by a circle of stone blocks, but these are not laid to form a continuous flat ring but are laid 'as they come' to form an uneven edge to the cairn. The cairn itself rises up immediately inside the encircling ring of stones. None of the bordered cairns have been excavated so we have no evidence of their inner structure, what their burial deposits consisted of, or of their date. They could be seen as primitive prototypes, contemporary 'poor relations', or later degenerate imitations of the kerbed cairns. For the most part they occur in isolation, although there are a couple of pairs.

This is in contrast to the kerbed cairns. The eight examples on Barra are in pairs, and on Vatersay we have two pairs, three foursomes, and one remarkable site where no less than nine kerbed cairns lay cheek by jowl. The kerbed cairns are a formally coherent group and look like carefully constructed monuments. To test that hypothesis and to understand how and when they were used for burial we excavated two of the examples on south Vatersay. They both stood on the headland that runs out to Huilish Point, separated from each other by a steep-sided little valley but clearly intervisible. We were surprised by what we found.

We can focus here on the more northerly cairn, known to us as VS4B. It was one of four cairns set in a more or less straight line; there may have been a fifth cairn close by. We had to excavate from top to bottom of course, but here it makes more sense to describe the sequence the other way round, which means in effect from start to finish in the cairn's history. Soil from beneath the kerbstones was fine, sandy and mostly stone-free, possibly cultivated, but pollen suggested that the cairn was surrounded by good quality grassland at the time it was built. An oval of small stone blocks about 2 metres by 1.5 metres had been laid on the natural soil, inside of which were some flat slabs lightly covered with a spread of small cobbles. Among these was an oval sandstone 'rubber' 14 cm long, the sort of implement normally used to grind corn on a quernstone. Sitting on top of all this was a deposit of burnt clayey soil flecked orange, red and black with small fragments of charred bone spread through it. It was the remains of a cremation pyre – but there was not much of it, no ash, and the stone forming the oval beneath it showed few signs of burning. This was a purely symbolic sample from a cremation pyre – the full cremation had taken place elsewhere.

Over the pyre material four flat slabs were laid and these were covered by a thin deposit of cultivated soil brought here from somewhere else for the purpose. This in turn was overlain by a spread of burnt cobbles and white

Debris from a cremation pyre on an oval platform of stones at the base of an excavated kerbed cairn (VS4B) on Vatersay.

beach pebbles, so there was now a small, low oval cairn. This was entirely covered by 5–10 cm of pure black soil. Now cairn-building properly took place. A ring of stone blocks about 4.5 metres in diameter was put in place and smaller stones were deposited inside the ring to begin to build a stone mound. While this operation was in progress a narrow stone slab over a metre long was brought to the site and it was laid on the cairn material with one end buried under the stone blocks enclosing the cairn. It was a stone quite unlike any other in the cairn, and if we had found it out in the open we would have identified it as a small but well-formed 'standing stone'.

Once the inner cairn had been built the larger and more regular blocks to be used for the kerb were laid out in a ring of nearly 8 metres in diameter. The space between the kerb and the inner cairn was infilled with a spread of irregular small stone blocks. Finally the whole monument was covered with a scattering of small fieldstones. Resting on these near the crest of the cairn we found a very regularly shaped piece of gneiss which looked like an axe with a bevelled edge. On one of the kerbstones we found another piece of shaped gneiss which looked like the stone plough tips used in the prehistoric northern isles. Neither of these items were the 'real thing' – they were imitations, never meant to be used and purely symbolic. Indeed the whole cairn seemed to be full of symbolism from its sample of pyre material, its buried standing stone, its deposits of beach pebbles, cultivated soil and fieldstones, to its three stone implements – a quern rubber, an imitation axe, and plough tip. Furthermore it was clear that far from being a simple monument, where a stone mound had been thrown over the remains of a cremation, this cairn was built to a preconceived plan involving up to a dozen successive and distinct phases of construction.

The excavation of VS4B raised several questions, some of which we were unable to answer. For example, if the cremation was not actually carried out at the cairn site, where had it taken place? The burnt beach pebbles collected, carried to the cairn, and placed immediately over the pyre material might suggest the cremation had been done on the beach, but it's no more than a possibility. Why was a layer of cultivated soil used to cover the small oval cairn? The quern rubber and imitation axe and plough tip are suggestive of a connection with agriculture, as is the scatter of small fieldstones which capped the cairn. So was the person commemorated by this cairn an agriculturalist rather than a sheep or cattle farmer? Most puzzling of all is the buried standing stone. A connection between standing stones, representative of ancestors, and a burial place is entirely logical and as we have already noted is clearly demonstrated at Dun Bharpa. But the whole point of a standing stone was to be conspicuous, to be seen, so why should this one be buried in a cairn where it would never be seen again?

There also remained one of the questions which had prompted us to excavate our two cairns in the first place – when were they constructed? We

An 'inner cairn' of stones surrounded by upright stone blocks at the core of the kerbed cairn VS4B.

were disappointed but not surprised that we had found no 'grave goods' which would point clearly to a date. Apart from the 'agricultural implements', the only artefacts we found were fifteen sherds of pottery and about twenty pieces of flint including two end-scrapers, two blades and two cores, none closely dateable. The pottery sherds could all have come from a single thick-walled vessel, similar perhaps to Middle/Late Bronze Age ones from South Uist – but without any rims or decorated sherds dating was difficult. There was one other find, however: a fragment of a bronze 'cloak-fastener' which was probably accidentally lost by someone helping to build the cairn. This is likely to have been of LBA date. We sent a sample of pottery, and a second sample from pottery of a different rather thinner fabric found in our other cairn, for 'Optically Stimulated Luminescence' dating. When the results came back they broadly confirmed the M/LBA date of our cairn, with brackets of 1450–650 BC, but suggested the other cairn was earlier – 2500–1500 BC. This is a particularly wide dating bracket, but it does suggest that our two cairns were probably built at least several centuries apart.

Cremations, for obvious reasons, do not normally provide much skeletal evidence for the people who were cremated. In the case of VS4B the fragments of bone found in the sample of pyre material were so small we could say nothing at all about the deceased. The sample of pyre material buried in the other cairn we excavated was a little more informative. It was possible to say that the cremation itself had reached a high temperature (over 600 °C), and that the deceased was a muscular and robust adult, probably but not

A kerbed cairn (VS4B) as it was completed, with a neatly laid outer kerb and a covering of small rocks and fieldstones.

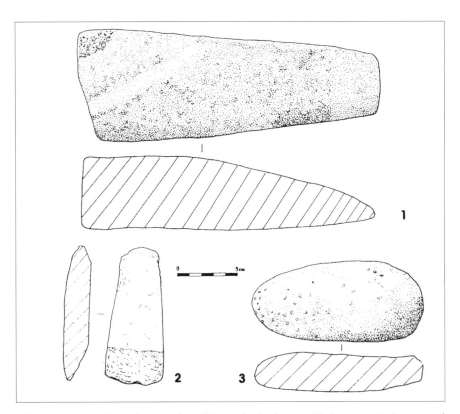

Three 'agricultural' implements found in the kerbed cairn VS4B: 1 – an imitation ard or plough tip, 2 – an imitation stone axe, 3 – a quern rubber.

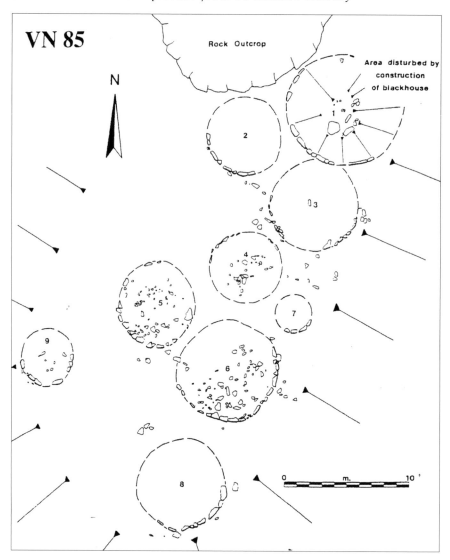

The remarkable 'cemetery' of nine kerbed cairns found in 'Death Valley' to the west of Tresivick.

certainly a man. Given the care and effort that went into the whole process, including building a good cremation pyre on islands which by this time had very few trees, we might wonder if cremation and a kerbed cairn were privileges extended to only a limited and therefore somewhat exclusive group of people. Certainly if our kerbed cairns were erected over a period of five or six centuries, even allowing for ones subsequently destroyed or unrecorded there were certainly nothing like enough to go round the whole population.

It is pure speculation as to which particular people were selected for the erection of a permanent memorial in the form of a cairn. It is natural for us to think perhaps in terms of the heads of family, so that the cairn cemetery in which VS4B sat would represent the burials of four, possibly five successive heads of a single family. But in that case we have to recognise that in the majority of cases, where cairns occur in pairs, the building of cairns lasted for no more than two generations. Were there perhaps other more exclusive criteria by which people were selected for this mode of burial and commemoration?

All of this speculation is thrown into further confusion by the discoveries we made on the opposite side of Bagh Siar (West Bay) on Vatersay. Here, in a small shallow valley we discovered no less than nineteen kerbed cairns in an area only about 250 metres square. We inevitably came to refer to this place as 'Death Valley'. All the cairns were on the east side of the stream which runs down the centre of the valley; to the west were remains of several roundhouses, although from surface indications we thought these were probably of Iron Age date. Even within this very limited area, the cairns formed clusters, a pair on the edge of the coast, four on a shelf halfway up the valley and four more on a shelf higher up. The remaining nine cairns were clustered together on a low hillock near the stream. The biggest was 9 metres in diameter and the smallest just 2.8 metres, with the rest ranging in between. We had noticed that in all the pairs and clusters we found, there were clear differences in size between the cairns, but that impression was emphasised at this site. Were the differences pure chance and unimportant, or did they reflect differences of status? Inevitably our smallest cairn – so much smaller than any other – raised speculations that it might be the grave of a child. We also wondered what the social relationship was between the people building cairns around the edge of the valley and those clustered on the hillock. Were they equals or in some way differentiated?

Even if all the cairns were excavated these questions, and others, would almost certainly remain unanswered. But our recognition of these monuments and the excavation of two of them have confirmed that, at least for a select handful of people, the living went to considerable trouble to bury and commemorate their dead in the proper manner. On Bronze Age Barra and its neighbouring islands, death was clearly an important part of life.

3

Tower Builders – Reaching for the Sky in the Iron Age

The pioneer settlement site at Allt Easdal was abandoned by the early second millennium BC, but elsewhere on Barra and Vatersay farmsteads were to be widely found by this time, apparently occupied by single families who lived in small circular stone and turf huts like the example excavated at Allt Easdal. These houses saw little change architecturally from 2500 BC down to the early years of the first millennium BC. An example excavated in the Borve valley and dated to the beginning of the Iron Age, perhaps 700 BC, was still only large enough for a small family to cluster round its hearth, but it was a little larger than its Neolithic ancestor, and its wall was notably thicker. Soon, however, much larger roundhouses began to spread across the landscape, with diameters of between 8 and 12 metres, and walls between 1 and 1.5 metres wide. If they still housed single 'nuclear' families, then they must have offered scope for the division of the interior into separate areas for different activities.

Nevertheless, the appearance in the first century BC of roundhouses up to 18–20 metres in diameter and, more dramatically, soaring 10–15 metres into the sky, must have been almost as much of a shock to the Iron Age population as it was to twentieth-century archaeologists. These remarkable towers, which archaeologists call 'brochs', surely must be the product of incoming, colonising foreigners. Furthermore, given the amount of labour involved in their construction, the intruders must have used the native people as forced labour to build their impregnable fortified towers. Some archaeologists suggested the invaders were native chieftains from southern Britain ousted by, and fleeing from, the Roman invaders. Others, noting that there were no structures remotely comparable to the brochs in England and Wales, believed they could only have been built by emigrants who had sailed up the western Atlantic seaboard from Iberia or the west Mediterranean, where stone-built towers of the first millennium BC could be found.

The basal gallery of the broch of Dun Ruadh, Pabbay, with a cross-slab still in situ.
(P. Foster)

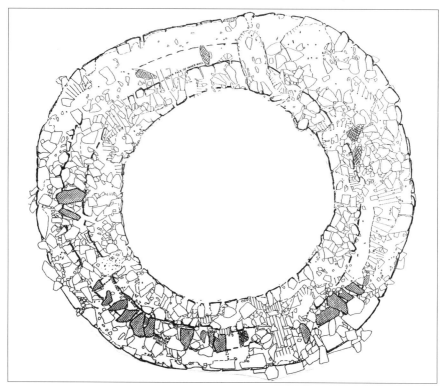

A measured plan of the Dun Caolis broch on Vatersay; note the shaded slabs which are the floor of the gallery at first-floor level. (C. Merrony)

Given the apparent architectural and conceptual gap between the simple roundhouses and the brochs, such ideas are perhaps understandable. The brochs were not simply monumental structures, but they were certainly much more sophisticated pieces of architecture than anything seen previously in the Western Isles. Their encircling wall was 4–5 metres wide at the base, but for most of their height the broch was enclosed in fact by two walls, each about 1.5 metres wide, with a metre-wide 'gallery' separating them. Within the thickness of the wall at ground level were small cellular rooms, but higher up the galleries gave access to a first-floor room reached by stone-built staircases within the wall. Some brochs probably had a further second floor, again reached by staircases, before the pitched timber roof was reached. The upper floors were supported by 'scarcement' ledges on the inner wall face, and some light and heat was allowed to percolate into the galleries by constructing 'voids', or internal windows, into the inner wall.

Despite these revolutionary developments, the idea that the brochs were built by more highly skilled and powerful incomers from 'the south' has now been abandoned. It had always seemed odd that incomers from more advanced and sophisticated cultures should adopt the material culture of the 'backward' indigenous population over which they were supposed to be lording it. Yet excavations of brochs repeatedly yielded the same sort of pots and pans, the same sort of bone and stone tools, and the same (very limited) range of iron and bronze objects that were found in the simpler roundhouses. Then excavations in the Orkneys in the later twentieth century uncovered a series of buildings dating from the centuries before the first brochs appeared which revealed architectural features being developed which were soon to be incorporated into broch architecture. These included very thick walls with intra-mural cells, stone stairs, and timber upper floors. Similar features were then found at two sites on Lewis at the northern end of the Western Isles, both dating to the pre-broch period. Today it is accepted that the broch towers were developed in the islands off the north and west coasts of Britain, and that they represent the ingenuity and skills of the indigenous people of these regions.

This was perhaps always suggested by the geographical distribution of the brochs which are found only in the Northern Isles, the Western Isles, and western Scotland. At least five brochs were built on Barra, and others on Vatersay, Sandray and Pabbay. All five of the Barra brochs, and that on Vatersay, are easily accessible to the modern-day visitor. At first sight none are very impressive because, like brochs throughout the region, they have been regarded as convenient sources of stone to be quarried by later generations and have been reduced to a shadow of their former glory. But all are worth visiting and on close inspection some provide vivid insights into their construction.

The broch situated on an islet at Airdveenish, with its tidal causeway revealed at low water.

The best preserved of the group is that on a low hill at Caolis on northern Vatersay. The outer wall face today stands little more than a metre high, but you should climb onto the wall itself and walk around its southern circuit and look at the stones beneath your feet. They are flat slabs which cross from the inner face of the outer wall, to the outer face of the inner. You are in fact walking along the floor of the first-floor gallery, which means that behind the mass of tumbled stone inside the broch, the walls probably still stand 2 metres high. At the south-west corner for a short distance a scarcement ledge is visible, which would have carried the supports for the timber floor at this level. Some idea of the investment of time and labour that went into building a broch is conveyed by the dense mass of collapsed stone blocks which had been hauled up the hill, and then built into two wide walls to a height of 10 metres or more. Walking around the outside face of the wall, one can also appreciate the care with which the wall was built and see the inclined batter of its face. On the south and south-east side some of the basal blocks of stone are up to 1.5 metres long, 0.9 metres wide and 0.6 metres deep. Dragging these up the hill, and then manoeuvring and lifting each of them into position, would have been a long and hard task for several strong men.

Not all brochs employed quite such massive masonry. The broch which stood on Borve headland and is now incorporated into the corner of the modern cemetery was built of more modest blocks and survives to a height of 2 metres and five courses. Inside the cemetery the collapsed masonry still forms a mound over 4 metres high, on which a small chapel was later built. What appears to be the original door of the broch can still be seen in the outside face, a tiny opening little more than half a metre wide and a metre in height. This would have been the only opening and feature to be seen on the outside face of the entire broch, emphasising the massive monumentality of the structure and presenting a forbidding appearance to those approaching it.

Equally impressive may have been the broch sitting on a small islet in the waters of Northbay at Airdveenish. The islet itself stands about 5 metres above the surrounding sea level, so that the broch which took up the entire summit of the islet would have appeared even taller than it really was. Although heavily overgrown the double encircling wall and narrow gallery are still visible, and in size this broch is similar to the others on Barra. The air of impregnability which the great tower conveyed here was amplified by the approach to the broch, which was not up a low hill or across a flat headland, but via a 20-metre-long, roughly built causeway which, today at least, is submerged by the sea at high tide.

The forbidding appearance of a broch in its prime has inevitably led to speculation that these towers were built as primarily defensive structures – miniature castles if you like – which served as a place of refuge when hostilities broke out between neighbouring groups or when raiders came sweeping up the western seaboard. The outer wall would have been all but

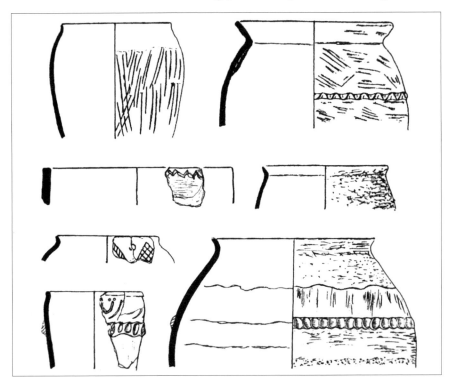

Pottery, mostly jars, with incised decoration and finger-impressed cordons, found in Dun Ruadh, Pabbay.

impossible to climb and far too thick to easily undermine. The tiny entrances were very easy to block and to defend. From the top of the wall the defenders would be able to attack those outside with impunity. As long as good supplies of food and water were laid in, a broch could be held against attack almost indefinitely.

Recently the defensive qualities of the brochs have been played down by archaeologists, and more emphasis has now been placed on their role as permanent homes. Excavations inside the broch towers, and in the rubbish dumps outside them, have revealed that they were indeed lived in on a permanent basis by families who in terms of their everyday activities and material culture were very similar to those living in contemporary roundhouses. They used exactly the same sort of rather heavy and poorly decorated pottery bowls, jars and buckets, carried out a limited amount of spinning and weaving wool, and iron- and bronze-working for simple tools and ornaments. Equally there is no doubt that they too were essentially farmers who raised stock and grew crops, as demonstrated by the plentiful animal bones and charred grain in their rubbish dumps.

But accepting that brochs were essentially permanently occupied farmhouses does not explain why they were built at the same time as, and often close to, simple roundhouses and another contemporary type of house, the wheelhouse. In terms of architectural complexity and investment of energy, the wheelhouse stands somewhere between the simple roundhouse and the broch. Its interior area is often much the same as that of the large simple thick-walled roundhouse and the central floor area of the brochs, but it is divided up by radial piers into small cells with corbelled ceilings. Some of the wheelhouses on Barra were built by digging a hole in the sandy machair and building a stone facing around the inside of it – a method of wheelhouse construction commonly adopted in the islands further north. But Barra has a number of wheelhouses which were built entirely above ground, on rocky hillsides where a subterranean house was not an option.

Two of these wheelhouses have been excavated, one at Tigh Talamhanta in Allasdale, and the other at Allt Easdal, just across the stream upslope from the site of the Neolithic settlement. This building is both accessible and visible and is well worth a visit. It has an enclosing wall 1.5 metres wide and 10 metres in diameter, with a door on the south side facing onto the sound of Vatersay. It was divided into six cells inside, and the whole of the central area was taken up by a stone-lined square hearth. The stone piers which divided the interior also served to support corbelled roofing around the perimeter, so that only the central area needed to be roofed with timber rafters. At Allasdale, burnt debris collapsed into the middle of the building suggested that this central area may have had heather thatch on a framework of spruce poles. There must have been a hole in this roof to let out smoke from the fire immediately below, for the hearth was large and had seen much use. That at the middle of the Allt Easdal wheelhouse was even bigger, nearly 2 metres square. We found it still piled high with ash which fell over the stone edges onto the floor beyond, conjuring up images of a roaring fire around which the family clustered during the long, stormy Hebridean nights.

Just as the wheelhouses are architecturally somewhere between the simple roundhouses and the brochs in terms of complexity and the amount of manpower they needed in construction, so they are numerically somewhere in between the brochs and roundhouses. On Barra and Vatersay, taking only certain or near-certain examples, there are six brochs, thirteen wheelhouses and thirty-one large thick-walled roundhouses. It is not unreasonable to suggest that this might reflect a 'social pyramid', with the brochs representing the upper echelon of local society.

There are perhaps three considerations which support this view. The first is that the brochs were certainly built to be seen and, indeed, to physically overlook other contemporary dwellings. They were not only by far the tallest buildings in north-west Britain, but most of them were built where they were conspicuous – on the summit of a low hill, on an islet in the middle of a loch, or on a headland.

The excavated Iron Age wheelhouse at Allt Easdal with its radial piers and its doorway on the far side from the camera.

The great stratified deposit of ash from the central hearth of the Allt Easdal wheelhouse.

The second consideration is that their builders and occupiers could obviously mobilise substantial workforces and command scarce resources. The quantity of stone needed to build a broch tower was far in excess of that needed for a large roundhouse or wheelhouse – at a rough calculation at least ten times as much. Given enough time, a nuclear family might manage to collect and move such a huge amount of stone without other assistance. But moving some of the massive basal blocks to the site would have required many hands, and so too would lifting many of even the more modest blocks into position as the walls rose ever higher. While rough blocks of gneiss were plentiful, the more slab-like stones which were needed for the roofing of the galleries would be at a premium – such blocks occur naturally only in small numbers on Barra. They would have to be sought out and transported over considerable distances. Even scarcer of course were supplies of timber. That needed for the roof might have been recovered as driftwood, but the 9–10-metre lengths of strong timbers needed to support the first- and possibly second-storey floors of the brochs are very unlikely to have been available in the quantities needed, if at all. In that case, the broch builders must have imported timber spars from the mainland, or perhaps from Ireland. All in all a broch represented a huge investment of labour and scarce materials, and the families who could mobilise or acquire such resources must have been powerful or wealthy, or both.

Finally, we should perhaps look more closely at the evidence for the diets of the broch dwellers, compared to that of the families living in roundhouses and wheelhouses. To do this we have to consider the evidence primarily of the animal bones found in the rubbish deposits associated with these houses. Small 'faunal samples' were recovered from the wheelhouse at Allasdale, from a probable roundhouse site on Sandray, a roundhouse or wheelhouse on Mingulay, and a broch on Pabbay. The evidence suggests that, in general terms, the families at all these sites enjoyed very similar diets. The most numerous animals were sheep, but in terms of meat production cattle may have been at least as important. Small numbers of pig and deer added variety to the meat diet, and fish and seabirds were also caught. Fish were mainly cod, saithe and pollack but also included sea bream, wrasse, ling, haddock, conger eel, and John Dory. Seals were also caught. Most of these fish could be caught inshore at one time or other of the year. Seabirds also contributed to the diet, particularly the shag, which in later times was favoured for making soups.

But these faunal samples from Barra and its adjacent islands were all too small to allow more detailed and reliable comparisons to be made between the diets of the roundhouse, wheelhouse and broch dwellers. A comparison of the faunal samples from fourteen wheelhouse or roundhouse sites and eight brochs elsewhere in the western isles, however, provides some interesting contrasts in the patterns of meat consumption. On average, the roundhouse and wheelhouse samples contained about 50 per cent sheep bones, 40 per

Ben Scurrival, like a miniature volcanic peak with a broch tower perched on its summit.

cent cattle, and 8 per cent pig. The broch samples had more cattle (47 per cent), fewer sheep (33 per cent) and more pig (18 per cent). The relatively high numbers of pig are significant because there is much evidence from Iron Age sites elsewhere in Britain that the pig was a favoured animal for feasting and was considered as high-status food. Cattle too seem to have had a higher status than sheep, and better reflected a families 'wealth'. So the faunal evidence suggests that broch dwellers consumed more of the valuable and high-status animals than the people living in the roundhouses and wheelhouses.

Taking all the evidence into account, then, it seems reasonable to conclude that the broch dwellers were at the top of the local social ladder. There are probably too many brochs to identify them as the homes of chieftains, but they may have been occupied by the heads of extended families or simply by local families which had achieved higher wealth and status than their neighbours.

For perhaps three or four centuries the brochs stood proud in the landscape of Barra and the other western isles, but pride comes before a fall and by the fourth century AD they had begun to fall into disrepair. Some were abandoned, but many saw smaller dwellings built in the shell of the broch tower. This happened at both Dun Cuier in Allasdale, and at Dun Ruadh on Pabbay. It seems that the broch dwellers were no longer able or willing to mobilise the resources necessary to maintain their towers, although the appearance of six bone dice in the ruins of Dun Cuier might tempt one to speculate that the owner here had lost his 'fortune' by gambling! Strangely, as the quality of the

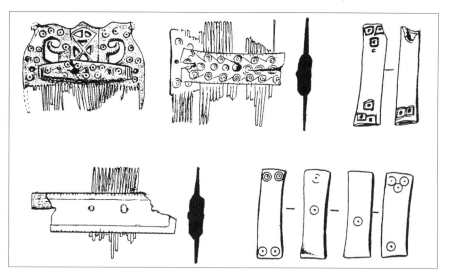

Decorated bone combs and dice from late occupation in the broch of Dun Cuier, Barra. (After A. Young)

architecture declined, the range and quality of items of personal adornment increased and improved. At Dun Cuier the most eye-catching items were decorated bone combs, while Pabbay yielded two fine bronze pins with elaborate terminals. Elsewhere bronze brooches, toilet tweezers, and glass beads were found in late broch occupation deposits. It was almost as if the broch dwellers were attempting to keep up appearances by dressing up.

4

Norsemen – Invaders in the Late First Millennium AD

In AD 793 the Vikings attacked and looted the monastery at Lindisfarne on the coast of Northumbria. Monasteries offered both rich pickings and soft targets, and just two years later the raiders descended on the monastery on Iona off the coast of Mull. In 799 they swept through the Hebrides on their way to attack Ireland, and they repeated attacks on Iona in 802 and 806. By this time the people of the Western Isles must have dreaded the appearance of the Viking longships on the horizon, although the raiders were mainly interested at this time in the richer prizes offered by monastic settlements and the Irish.

Nevertheless, the Vikings must have sought refuge from storms, fresh supplies of food, and whatever else they could carry off from brief visits to the Uists and Barra. In the Grettir Saga we learn the names of the first five Norsemen to visit Barra. The most important was Onund Woodenleg, whose story was recorded at length in the Saga. Onund arrived in Barra with five ships in AD 871. He was the son of Ofeig Clumsyfoot (disability seemed to run in the family!). He was accompanied by Balki, Orm, Halvard and Sugandi who each, presumably, commanded one of the ships in his squadron. Having defeated an Irish king, Kjarval, Onund and his companions decided to set up base in Barra as a convenient place from where they could raid Ireland. They stayed for three years, during which time they saw off other Viking raiders who attempted to attack Barra. In 874 Onund and his companions sailed off back home to Norway, but Onund was obviously a restless soul, and he eventually set out across the north Atlantic to settle and die in Iceland.

Although the first Vikings to come to Barra were little more than pirates who had no intention of settling in the Western Isles in the long term, some seem to have taken wives and one of these, Alfdis of Barra, is mentioned in the Grettir Saga. Scattered through the Inner and Outer Hebrides are the burials of some of these early Viking raiders and their wives. One of these of particular interest to us is found not on Barra but on the small island of

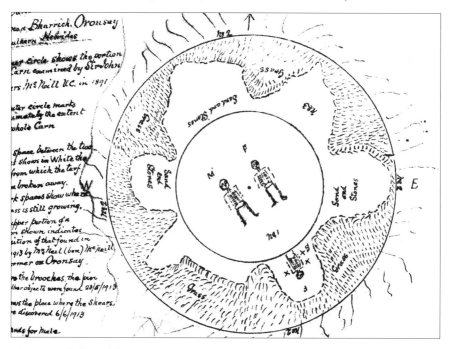

The original plan of the Norse burials in the cairn known as Carn a Bharraich, on the islet of Oronsay, Mull. (After S. Grieve)

Oronsay south of Mull. It is thought to be one of the earliest Norse burials in Scotland, and was found under a low mound just above the beach on the east side of the island. On the summit of the mound two thin slabs of stone had originally been set upright, and when the cairn was excavated two burials were found laid alongside one another at its centre, one an elderly man and the other a woman. The man had been buried accompanied by little more than an iron knife, but the woman was laid to rest with a remarkable array of personal belongings. In addition to beads of amber and serpentine (two materials commonly found on Viking sites) she had a bronze ringed-pin to hold her dress in place, and two impressive brooches made of gilt bronze with elaborate interlaced decoration. The really interesting thing about these brooches is that they had clearly been made by modifying the hinge-plate of a reliquary or book-shrine. That is, they were made from an item which had been looted from a Christian monastery or church. Could the man buried here have been one of those who had attacked Iona? A third burial was found to one side of the cairn, with another woman who again was buried with a ringed-pin and two bronze brooches as well as a pair of shears, and a small bronze needle-case – presumably a treasured possession.

Somewhat similar female burials, always with a pair of oval brooches, have been found in the Western Isles in Lewis and Harris, and one on Barra itself, of which more will shortly follow. But the particular interest of the Oronsay burials for Barra is the name which local tradition gave to the cairn which covered them – Carn a Bharraich, 'Cairn of the Barra men'. Clearly the people of Oronsay believed that the people buried here had originally come from the Isle of Barra on the other side of the Minches.

The burial found on Barra has remarkable similarities to that found on Oronsay. It was discovered and excavated in the 1860s by Commander Edge at a place which he called Ardvouray. This is almost certainly his English understanding of the local name for the Borve headland. Commander Edge described the burial place as being under a mound of sand with a standing stone on top of it, and on the sandy machair by the headland one can still see the remains of two standing stones, the better preserved of which was recorded a century ago as standing 2.9 metres high. From the burial Edge recovered the skeleton of an adult accompanied by two oval brooches of late eighth-century manufacture, a ringed-pin, a composite bone comb (made of three bone plates riveted together), a pair of heckles (for teasing out wool), a pair of shears, and an iron 'sword'. This last item persuaded Commander Edge that this was the burial of a Viking warrior, but in fact it was a 'weaving sword' used at the loom rather than on the battlefield, and the whole assemblage is clearly that of a woman. It is clearly very similar in content, situation, and use of stone grave markers, to the Oronsay burial.

These scattered burials are the best evidence we have for the early Norsemen in the Western Isles, and presumably represent those who were unfortunate

The burial mound on Pabbay with early (pre-Norse?) cross-slabs and a Christianised Pictish symbol stone (in front of the figure at the base of the mound). (P. Foster)

enough to die far from their homeland whether as a result of battle, natural causes, or accident. But gradually the Norsemen began to settle in the islands and to intermarry with the indigenous inhabitants. The increasing domination of the Norsemen led the kings of Norway to claim the islands as their own, but it is best reflected by the survival to this day of thousands of Norse place names throughout the Western Isles. All the Barra islands have names given to them by the Norsemen. Berneray, Mingulay, Pabbay, Sandray, Vatersay, Barray and Eriskay (as well as many smaller islands like Fuday, Hellisay, and Flodday) all end with the Norse 'ey', meaning island. Berneray, Barra and Eriskay were all named after prominent occupants of these islands – namely Bjorn, St Barr, and Eric. On each island there are a plethora of further much more localised place names. In Lewis and Harris many of these names include elements such as *byr, setr* and *stadir* referring to various types of settlement. Other common elements like *fjall, nes* and *vik* describe topographical features. There are so many Norse place names in the Western Isles that it has always been assumed these must reflect very extensive colonisation by the Norsemen in the tenth and eleventh centuries. A recent programme of DNA testing confirmed that many Hebrideans today do indeed have Norse blood in their veins.

Yet until a decade ago the number of Norse-period houses known from the Western Isles could be counted on the fingers of one hand, and not much more than a dozen sites had yielded pottery identified as Norse. From the handful of sites already found, however, it was clear that if archaeologists were looking for the classic Norse longhouse with bowed sides, shaped something like a

A Norse rectangular house under excavation on the machair at Bornish, South Uist. (M. Parker Pearson)

longship, then they would probably look in vain. Hebridean Norse houses were more sub-rectangular, sometimes with a hint of residual 'bowing' of the long walls. Archaeological survey by my colleague Mike Parker Pearson has now revealed two dozen low settlement mounds on South Uist which were occupied in the Norse period. Excavations at Kilpheder and Bornish have exposed a sequence of houses, each of which was built by lining a sub-rectangular flat-bottomed pit in the sand with drystone walling and building the walls proper with turf. The houses each had a long central hearth in the Norse tradition.

On Barra we still have to find such mounds and buildings, but at least we know where we should look – namely on the machair. On Barra this means the low pastures at Borve, Allasdale and Cuier on the west coast and the extensive machair pastures of the Eoligarry peninsula at the north end of the island. Borve has already produced the Norse burial we described earlier, and there are local stories of Viking burials with swords found near Craigston school. Islanders will also point out the great long mound of sand at south Allasdale, below which a Viking longboat is buried according to local tradition. But archaeological and geophysical survey in recent years has been unable to confirm either of these stories.

More local stories of the Norsemen on Barra focus on the Eoligarry peninsula. A Macneil of Barra is himself said to have fought and defeated an invading Viking who had landed on the great tidal beach at Traigh Mhor. The dead man was buried where he fell and a stone monument erected over

The island of Fuday, seen from Eoligarry, where tradition has it that the last Vikings on Barra were killed. Burials thought to be Norse were found on the island in the nineteenth century.

his grave. Across the narrow strip of machair which separates east and west coasts at this point, the body of a beautiful lady, no less than a daughter of the King of Norway, is said to have been found on the beach at Traigh Eias. Her body was buried beneath a mound on the spot where Eoligarry school now stands.

As for the last of the Norsemen on Barra, according to local tradition all three were finally slain on the island of Fuday just off the tip of the Eoligarry peninsula. Burials are said to have been found here after a storm in the nineteenth century, and local tradition again ascribes them to the Vikings, but too little is known about them to be sure.

Is there any archaeological evidence to suggest that these stories at least reflect a Norse presence in Eoligarry? A little, but not much. In a short visit to Fuday in 1992 my colleague Patrick Foster noted a round cairn with a standing stone on its summit – reminiscent of the Borve and Oronsay Norse burial cairns with their upstanding burial markers.

On the Eoligarry peninsula our surveys have discovered low settlement mounds like those on Uist but the sherds scattered across them do not look like Norse-period pottery. A small fragment of decorated bronze sheet found here in survey may be Norse, however. On the little island of Orosay just north of the airfield at Traigh Mhor an eroding midden has yielded half a dozen fragments of thin pottery which look very much like the 'platter ware' used to make baking plates in the Viking settlements on South Uist.

A denuded cairn with an upright stone marker recalling the Oronsay cairn, on Fuday. (P. Foster)

There is one burial site at the north end of the island, however, which certainly attests to a Norse presence, and even gives us the names of two more Barra Vikings. In the cemetery which surrounds the ancient church of Cille Bharr, named after the island's patron saint, a fine Celtic cross-slab nearly 1.4 metres tall was found in 1865. It dates to the late tenth century AD. Attractive as the interlaced cross and flanking spirals and meander patterns are, the real interest of this stone is found on the reverse face. Here there is a Viking inscription written in runic. Although the exact reading, and therefore its translation, is still uncertain, it is thought to read: 'After Thorgerth, Steinar's daughter, this cross was raised.'

One would love to know more about Steinar and his beloved daughter but it is unlikely we ever shall. We cannot even be certain that Thorgerth was actually buried at Cille Bharr. But corroborative evidence that Christian Norsemen were interred here may come from two small cruciform grave markers with incised crosses found in the cemetery. Not only are very similar crosses found in Norse-period cemeteries in Shetland, but the recent excavation at Kilpheder on South Uist discovered two bone pendants of similar shape in the Norse houses there.

Overall there is certainly sufficient evidence to confirm the presence of Vikings on Barra, and to suggest that one centre of Norse settlement was probably on the Eoligarry peninsula. Nevertheless the scarcity of identified Norse settlements on Barra, even after Parker Pearson has demonstrated how to find them and what we should be looking for, is still perplexing. It has been suggested that the solution to the puzzle may be discovered by a closer look at Norse place names on Barra.

We mentioned earlier the many place names in Lewis and Harris which had Norse elements relating to various types of settlement. These elements are almost entirely missing on Barra, the only exception perhaps being Borve. Otherwise the Barra place names use Norse elements which refer to topographical features or to places associated with animal husbandry. For example, *nes* (headland, e.g. Bruernish), *vagr* (bay, harbourage e.g. Bagh Hirivagh or Northbay), *vik* (a small bay e.g. Brevig), and *fjall* (a hill e.g. Heaval) are all features of the landscape which would be important to seamen. The elements *studhull* (milking place, e.g. Tangusdale and Allasdale) and *erg* (a shieling, e.g. Earsary and Skallary) were important to people herding cattle and sheep. The dominance of these place-name elements and the absence of those referring to settlements might perhaps reflect the nature of Norse interest in Barra. On the one hand it may have been regarded as a useful landfall and refuge for seamen moving between Ireland and the bigger, densely colonised islands to the north. On the other it may have had only a small permanent Norse population who were essentially pastoralists.

As it happens the only Viking-period occupation sites yet excavated on Barra lend some support to this theory. At Allt Easdal, where the first pioneers

The runic inscription on the back of the Celtic cross-slab found at Cille Bharra. It commemorates a Viking woman named Thorgerth. (D. Savory)

had settled and a fine wheelhouse had been built in the age of the tower builders, a flimsy little hut was found perched on the collapsed masonry of the wheelhouse. Its rectangular wall was constructed of stones pulled from the mass of rubble and enclosed an area only 2.5 metres by 1.7 metres. Its floor was trampled soil on which small fires had been lit at one end, and into the surface of which were trodden a handful of small sherds of pottery which were not diagnostically helpful, a few tiny flakes of flint, and a steatite spindle whorl. Study of the wear patterns on the flint flakes suggested they had been used as strike-a-lights and supported the evidence of the steatite spindle whorl and the stratigraphy that this little structure was a temporary hut used by a Norse-period shepherd.

At the same time as this structure was being excavated by Patrick Foster, I was excavating an interesting site tucked away in a small valley which runs down from the bleak and boggy Pass of the Mouth to an inlet north of Easary. It had been chosen for excavation because it clearly had at least three successive structures built one on top of the other. Such sites often provide the key to understanding at least the relative date of some of the varied types of small hut used on Barra for millennia. The uppermost structure was a simple shepherds' shelter marked out by a ring of stone blocks, enclosing an area 2 metres by 1.5 metres. A fireplace was found to one side of it. It was probably built and used within the last hundred years. Beneath it was a larger hut with a proper stone-faced wall enclosing an area of 2.3 metres by 1.7 metres, with a threshold slab on the north side, and a hearth area just inside the door. Next to this hut was a second two-roomed structure with a small oval room behind a U-shaped room, the whole structure measuring 5 metres by 2 metres internally. The only finds in either hut were two small sherds of handmade pottery and a flint flake. They provide no clue to the date of the structure, but it was clearly in an abandoned and collapsed state and largely overgrown when the overlying hut was built.

Beneath this complex, and partly destroyed by it, was a single substantial oval hut, with a wall over a metre wide. Built on quite a steep slope, the wall on the downhill side of the hut was built entirely of stone and survived to five courses, almost a metre high. On the upslope side the wall had only stone facing slabs, its core being of small lumps of turf. At the north-east corner there was a narrow doorway, only 0.5 metres wide, with a very worn threshold slab. The interior of the hut measured 5 metres by 4 metres and was divided into two areas by a stone wall foundation which ran in an arc from the east side just inside the door. The north end of the hut had a trampled earth floor and yielded a few scraps of handmade pottery. But the south end was much more interesting. The partition wall, which we believe was probably built up in turf on its stone foundation, proved to run along the edge of a low rock face about 30 cm deep, so that the area to the south was in fact a sunken area. In the north-east corner of this sunken area three upright blocks of stone

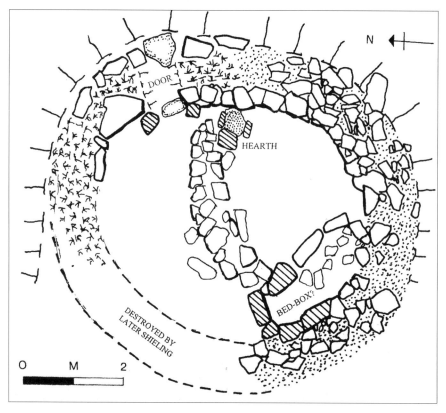

Plan of a Norse-period sheiling hut excavated at Ben Gunnary – 'Gunnar's sheiling'.

outlined a hearth area. On the opposite, west side, was a rectangular cist-like arrangement of stones 2.2 metres long, with five large blocks set upright around its northern end.

The sunken area gradually filled up with soil and this produced various types of material of interest to us. Pollen extracted from it revealed the presence of heather and ferns, which might have been brought into the hut for bedding. About three dozen pieces of pottery were found, including at least one piece with grass marking, and a similar quantity of pieces of flint were found. On close study these proved to be typical strike-a-lights used for lighting fires. Finally, just the day after Patrick Foster found his steatite spindle whorl in the little shieling hut at Allt Easdal we found an identical whorl in our hut. So we believe that this hut was a Norse-period shieling hut. It was rather more sophisticated than that perched on top of the old wheelhouse at Allt Easdal. Not only did it have thick, wind-proof walls, but the narrow doorway and internal partition would have helped to keep out wind and rain and the sunken area with its hearth might have been almost snug. And the rectangular stone setting to one side we believe was used as a bed box, filled with ferns or heather, and with the head-end protected by the upright draft excluders!

Amazingly we might, just might, know the name of the Norseman who slept in this bed. The slope on which the hut was built is the south-facing slope of a low hill which to this day carries the name Ben Gunnary. This name owes nothing to Ben Gunn of Robinson Crusoe fame. It is one of those Norse place names ending in *erg* or *ary*, which means a shieling, and Gunnary means 'Gunnar's shieling'. The hut we excavated was the only one found on Ben Gunnary, and we like to think that it was occupied by Gunnar the Norseman.

5

Outlaws – Treason, Piracy, and Raiding in the Middle Ages

After the Norsemen came the Macneils. There is much debate, and certainly no firm answer, as to when the Macneils set foot on Barra. Clan tradition has it that they arrived with Niall, son of Aodh Aonrachan, during the reign of King Malcolm II, sometime around AD 1030. Others place it much later, either in the later fourteenth century, or specifically in AD 1427, when the Lord of the Isles granted a charter to Gilleonan Macneil. But the granting of a charter seems more likely to be confirmation that the Macneils were firmly established on the island rather than their being new arrivals. The Clan Macneil in any event trace their ancestry back way beyond even 'Niall of the Castle' as he was dubbed by Robert Lister Macneil, the forty-fifth chief of the clan. They claim descent from the near legendary Irish King Niall of the Nine Hostages, who died at the beginning of the fifth century. In 1771, the Reverend John Walker said the then chief was 'in possession of vouchers for about 30 descents'. In fact, the teenage Roderick Macneil was hailed at that time by the clan as their fortieth chief.

The Macneils seem to have broadly conformed to the pattern of behaviour which was becoming established among the clans of the highlands and islands as a whole in the middle ages. The cement which held them together was the idea of kinship and the obligations that this laid both on the chief and his clansmen. The chief was expected to protect both his people and their territory, while they in turn gave him unswerving loyalty, paid him dues, and took up arms in his service. Territory and power were maintained and expanded by ever-shifting political and marriage alliances, while prestige and status were upheld by successful raids on other clans and by the provision of lavish feasts. Successive Macneils of Barra did all of these things with varying degrees of relish and success and, according to several contemporary sources, with a good deal of pride. More than a century after Kisimul Castle had been abandoned, the tale was still told how, every evening, Macneil's herald would climb to the top of the castle's tower and proclaim, 'Hear oh ye people, and listen oh ye nations. The great Macneil having finished his meal, the princes of the earth may dine.'

Pride, raiding, and the constantly changing patterns of clan alliances inevitably led the Macneils into falling foul of the Scottish kings who, after the Battle of Largs in 1263, claimed the Western Isles for the Scottish state and expected submission and obedience from the clans who inhabited them. Indeed, at the Battle of Largs itself, Macneil of Barra and his men are said to have fought alongside King Haakon of Norway against Alexander III of Scotland. Be that as it may, at Bannockburn in 1314, Niall Og, twenty-sixth chief of the Clan Macneil, fought with Robert the Bruce against the English.

Traitors

From the mid-fourteenth century to the mid-sixteenth century, however, only two of the ten chiefs of the clan are not recorded as having at some time in their chieftainship become, in effect, outlaws. Niall Og's son and heir, Muirceartach, set the pattern by refusing to pay taxes to the Scottish king or to attend his parliament. His own son and successor, Roderick (XXVIII) likewise refused King James's invitation to attend his parliament at Inverness – a wise move as it turned out, for those clan chiefs who did attend were seized and imprisoned by the king. Gilleonan (XXIX) and Roderick (XXX) are not known to have transgressed the king's law, though both owed their first allegiance to the Lord of the Isles. But Gilleonan (XXXI) and King James IV had a tempestuous relationship. Initially, all was well. In 1495 James confirmed the charter for Barra and Boisdale (in South Uist) given to Gilleonan's grandfather in 1427. But just three years later the Macneil and other chiefs were told their charters were no longer valid and they would have to pay up to have them restored. The clans formed an alliance against the king, led by a Macleod and a Maclean. When the alliance collapsed, the king charged Macneil and others with the task of apprehending Maclean of Duart and the destruction of his lands. But the Macleans and the Macneils were old allies, and when Macneil refused to act against the Macleans he was summonsed for treason against the crown in 1503, 1504 and 1505.

The rebels were finally brought to book and pardoned, but Gilleonan's successor as Macneil of Barra – another Gilleonan (XXXII) – supported a rebel 'Lord of the Isles' against the king in 1513, and yet again joined an alliance to attack the king's ally, the Campbells, in 1529. On both occasions he was forced to submit, but he managed to retain his freedom. But in 1540 he and other rebel chiefs were lured aboard the king's fleet and were carried off to imprisonment in Edinburgh and Dunbar. They remained there until the king died in 1543. Once released, the Hebridean chiefs, including the new Macneil (Gilleonan XXXIII) came out in support of Henry VIII against the Scottish

King James IV of Scotland, who had a tempestuous relationship with the Macneils of Barra. (Courtesy of National Galleries of Scotland)

crown. Inevitably Macneil was again declared a traitor and summonsed for treason no less than seven times in the space of twelve months! Having eventually been pardoned, he was once more declared a rebel against the king in 1579, following complaints by the Bishop of the Isles that Macneil was preventing him from collecting dues, and from going about his lawful business.

Gilleonan died shortly afterwards, to be succeeded by his son Roderick, known as Rory Og. Rory Og Macneil (XXXIV) soon joined with the clan's old allies the Macleans in attacking the Macdonalds, and shortly after in the 'treasonable burning and destruction of the islands of Rhum, Canna and Eigg'. He was pardoned in 1589, and again in 1592. Rory Og was succeeded by the most famous, or some might say infamous, of the Macneils of Barra, variously known as Roderick the Turbulent or Rory the Tartar.

In 1605 Rory was ordered to deliver up his castle as a guarantee of his clan's future good behaviour. If he failed to remove himself and his household from Kisimul within twenty-four hours it would be besieged and he would be declared a traitor. He ignored the demand, but the following year Mackenzie of Kintail was given a commission to 'take and slay' Macneil of Barra. He failed, and in 1607 Rory the Tartar joined in further ferocious attacks on the lowland colonists on Lewis. The king was furious and commanded the Earl of Huntly to 'extirpate and rute out' Macneil and Clanranald. But Rory remained at freedom, and wisely chose to ignore a summons to attend a court

The coat of arms of the Macneil of Barra showing a galley with furled sails at lower left.

held by the Lieutenant of the Isles in Mull. Those chiefs who went were seized and incarcerated in Stirling and Dumbarton castles. Rory continued to be a thorn in the king's side, and an order for his arrest was again issued in 1610 for his barbarous activities and rebellion. Ironically, Rory the Tartar ended up imprisoned in Kisimul Castle not by the agents of the king, but by his own son, Neil Og, who kept him incarcerated until his death.

By this time Neil Og (XXXVI Macneil) had already been declared a rebel and he initially followed in his father's footsteps in raiding and rebellion. But in his old age he supported the Stuarts against Cromwell and thereafter, for a hundred years, when the Macneils rebelled, it was against the crown of England.

I have recorded these three hundred years of Macneil rebellion against the crown in some detail to emphasise that it was a firmly entrenched pattern of behaviour (which was of course shared by some of the other highland clans too). They were fiercely independent and resented attempts by the powers that be on the mainland to curb their activities, take taxes, and generally interfere in their way of life. It is an attitude which did not die with Neil Og in the mid-seventeenth century. In 1690 a royal emissary to Kisimul complained that he had been greeted with a barrage of stones and over eighty shots aimed at him from 'guns, pistolls, muskets' and various other weapons. The Macneil of Barra he said showed 'a high and proud contempt of His Majesty's authority'.

Pirates

Political alliances against the king and other forms of rebellion, however, were not the only ways in which the Macneils put themselves beyond the law in the middle ages. The Macneils earned a reputation for piracy which reached its zenith under the chieftainship of Rory the Tartar. Kisimul Castle had a galley house just outside its gateway, and a short length of its wall can still be seen to the left of the gateway into the castle. This two-storey building housed the crew of the Macneil's black galley, in which he roamed the seas in search of lucrative targets. Many ballads refer to Macneil's galley, and the galley figures prominently both on the Macneil coat of arms and on one of the late medieval grave-slabs preserved in the chapel at Cille Bharra.

Rory the Tartar preyed on French and Dutch ships sailing through the Minches or down the Atlantic seaboard, but also ventured into the Irish Sea and attacked English and Spanish vessels too. After one such attack, Queen Elizabeth demanded that King James bring Rory to justice. The king commissioned Roderick Mackenzie of Kintail to carry out the arrest of Macneil. Mackenzie resorted to trickery, sailing into Castlebay, posing as the skipper of a barque which had just managed to purchase some fine French wines from a passing merchantman. Macneil was invited to come aboard

An elaborately decorated grave-slab in Cille Bharra, reputed to have been brought back to Barra as loot following a raid on Iona. (S. Boutell)

to sample the wines, and predictably overindulged. When he was helplessly drunk, Mackenzie battened down the hatches and sailed off with Rory the Tartar safely secured. He was taken before the king in the palace of Holyrood, and when asked to explain his behaviour he told James that he thought he was doing the king a favour by plundering the subjects of the queen who had executed the king's mother (Mary Queen of Scots). James thereupon released him, but awarded the superiority of Barra to Mackenzie, to whom Rory was obliged to pay an annual duty of 40 merks.

The episode did not prevent Rory from pursuing his piratical career, however. Late in 1609 a Bordeaux-based merchant by the name of Abel Dynes made the mistake of putting into Castlebay while carrying a cargo of fine Spanish wine. The Macneils, led by Rory's son John Og, seized the vessel, killing or wounding five of the crew in the process. In due course John Og was taken prisoner and hauled off to be incarcerated in the Tolbooth prison in Edinburgh. When John Og died there, a renewed charge of piracy was laid against his brother Neil. Abel Dynes was persistent, if nothing else, and the prosecution dragged on until 1613, when the case was finally dropped, by which time Rory the Tartar and his sons' reputation as the most active pirates in the Western Isles had been firmly and irrevocably established.

Raiders

The galleys which enabled the Macneils to practise piracy also carried them far afield on raiding parties. We have already mentioned the raids they carried out against the lowland colonists of Lewis, and their murderous attacks on the Macdonalds of Rum, Canna and Eig. Although these attacks were mounted to settle political scores between the clans, they were no doubt used as an opportunity to loot and steal, as well as to kill and destroy. But the Macneils also carried out raids, particularly against Ireland, whose sole purpose was to seize moveable wealth in whatever form it was found. In the same year that they attacked the Macdonalds of Rum, the Macneils raided Co. Mayo, slaughtering 600 cattle and carrying off 500 hides. They repeatedly attacked the coast of Connaught, and were warned by Act of Parliament in 1594 to stop their cattle-stealing practices. The Dean of Limerick was moved the following year to declare that 'Macneil of Barra [is] reputed the best sea-faring warrior in the islands'.

Looters

Sometimes, fortune smiled on the Macneils and booty simply fell into their lap. The western seaboard of Scotland is littered with the wrecks of ships driven by fierce storms onto the unforgiving rocks that are found along the coasts of the islands and mainland alike. Many of these ships carried cargoes that were worth risking life and limb to seize, not least the ships of the Spanish Armada in 1588. But though the *San Juan de Sicilia* went down in Tobermory Bay on Skye, and many of the Armada were wrecked on the coast of Ireland, none are known to have gone down around Barra. Nevertheless Barra has had its fair share of wrecks, the most famous (actually wrecked off nearby Eriskay) being the SS *Politician* of Whiskey Galore fame. A late sixteenth-century Dutch trading vessel – name unknown – went down off Fuday, and in 1636 the *Susannah* from France, bound for Limerick, went down off Barra. The Macneils towed the ship into harbour but before they could carry off the cargo were confronted by 300 of Clanranald's men. In the face of overwhelming odds, the Macneils stood aside and allowed the men from South Uist to seize the vessel and its contents.

But it was the wrecking of the Dutch East Indiaman the *Adelaar* (Eagle) off Greian headland on the west side of the island on the night of 24 March 1728 that provides the most interesting and amusing example of the race to recover the cargo of a shipwrecked vessel off the coast of Barra. The *Adelaar* was only six years old when it went down. It had left the Netherlands on 21 March, carrying 220 souls, which included a company of sixty soldiers and about 120 seamen. The rest of the complement were company officials and their families and a handful of other passengers. The ship's hold was packed with a general cargo of cloth, ironmongery and tools, and 'paying ballast' of bricks and lead

The reef off Greian headland where the Dutch ship the *Adelaar* was wrecked with the loss of all lives in 1728. (C. Martin)

ingots. But because the main purpose of the voyage was to purchase and bring
back to Europe quantities of tea, spices and fine tableware the ship also took
on board 500 bars of silver, six bars of gold, and nearly half a million coins
packed into seventeen chests, each of which was secured with two padlocks.

On the night of Sunday 24 March a severe storm blew up with fierce winds
from the north-north-west. The *Adelaar* was initially driven into Scurrival
bay, and then, attempting to get out to sea again, it was driven onto a reef just
off Greian headland. Neither the ship nor its passengers stood a chance. The
ship sank into a deep gully, and all 220 souls were lost. Debris, some of the
lighter items of cargo, and the bodies of some of the passengers were found
the next morning by villagers. The Macneil of Barra, Roderick the Dove of
the West (as he was known), was by chance away from home, visiting Harris
at the other end of the island chain. But a messenger was instantly dispatched
and within forty-eight hours Roderick had returned to Barra. He knew
that he and his people had to work fast before the authorities learnt of the
disaster and intervened, the authorities in this case being locally represented
by Macdonald of Boisdale on South Uist. Roderick therefore posted guards at
the ferry landing from South Uist with strict orders that no one was to enter
or leave the island.

Over the next seven days the locals collected whatever they could find
washed up on the shore with each tide, including any valuables found on
the bodies of passengers and crew. But the wreck itself was in too dangerous
and exposed a location for them to try and remove anything from its hold.
Meanwhile Macdonald had become suspicious that no one was coming across
the sound of Barra to South Uist, and when ship's timbers began to be washed
up on his beaches he sent a ship to investigate. Once he received news of the
shipwreck he immediately filled three boats with his clansmen and sailed to
Barra, where he confronted Macneil and demanded the return of everything
that had been collected from the ship. Macneil, knowing he had no legal leg
to stand on, told Macdonald he could indeed take everything that had been
recovered from the *Adelaar*, which would of course include all the now naked
but still unburied bodies that had been deposited on the beach at Greian. In
the end Macdonald thought better of it and agreed that the Macneils could
keep one-third of the items recovered, but that the rest should be transferred
initially to South Uist. However, not a single inhabitant of the island could be
found who admitted to possessing anything from the *Adelaar*, or knowing of
anyone else who did.

Macdonald subsequently sent a full report to the Admiral Depute in
Edinburgh, who sent someone to Barra to carry out further investigations. He
recovered some documents which had been washed ashore, and it was only
when these were examined back in Edinburgh that the nature of the rich cargo
of the *Adelaar* was finally recognised. There followed a remarkable salvage
operation, using a 'diving engine', which eventually enabled the recovery of

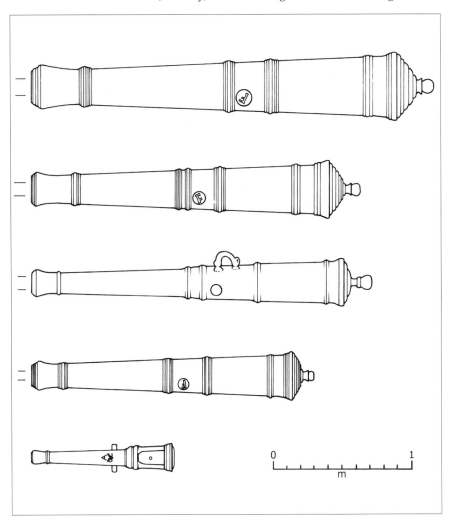

Some of the *Adelaar*'s guns, recovered by marine archaeologists in the 1970s. (C. Martin)

most of the silver, gold and coinage from the ship. During these operations, a disgruntled Macneil, aware of just what wealth had been almost within his grasp, managed to salvage a little pride and a modest profit by selling food and boats to the expedition at inflated prices.

The final chapter in the story of the *Adelaar* was only written in the 1970s when the Scottish Institute of Maritime Studies undertook an underwater excavation of the site, recovering some of the ship's guns, some of the lead ingots which she had carried as ballast, and a small collection of ironmongery. In addition they found three fine gold finger-rings and a pair of gold buttons, the property of either senior officers or wealthy passengers on the ship, and a poignant reminder of the human tragedy which the wreck of *Adelaar* represented.

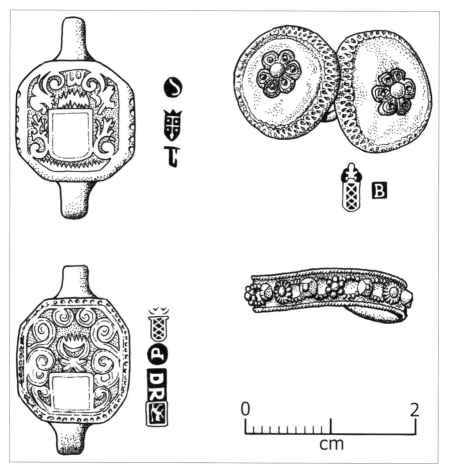

Gold rings and buttons from the *Adelaar*, found during her underwater excavation in the 1970s. (C. Martin)

6

Jacobites – Fighting a Lost Cause in the Seventeenth and Eighteenth Centuries

Following the foundation of the monastery on Iona by St Columba in the mid-sixth century AD, Irish monks brought Christianity to the Western Isles. These monks lived simple lives with few earthly trappings, so they left little physical trace of their existence. But some Norse place names are thought to commemorate their presence in the islands, and one of these is Barra itself. There is still debate as to whether or not the Norse name means the island of (St) Barr, but it is probably the most convincing explanation. If it is true, then it means that the surviving twelfth-century chapel at Cille Bharra was probably preceded by an earlier building dating back to the mid-ninth century, before the arrival of Onund Woodenleg. Similarly, the small island south of Sandray still known as Pabbay is thought to have been so called by the Vikings because it was the home of a Christian priest. Simple cross-marked burial slabs found in the cemetery there may have been erected in the pre-Norse period.

As both Norse settlers and surviving native islanders adopted the Christian faith in succeeding centuries, small chapels were built elsewhere in the southern isles. In 1549 Dean Munro claimed that there were chapels on all the populated islands south of Barra, but only those on Vatersay and Mingulay have any certain traces surviving to this day. Cille Bharra itself became an important religious focus and additional chapels were built there. To what extent these various chapels fell into decay as a result of the Reformation in the reign of Henry VIII is uncertain, but even Cille Bharra was recorded as being roofless in 1625.

However, the Reformation seems not to have had any major impact in the Western Isles and clashes between Catholics and followers of the reformed church were few. One of the rare exceptions occurred on Barra in 1609, however, when the Protestant parson, John Macneil, was slain by Macdonald of Benbecula. Even this event, however, may have had more to do with personal and family feuding than religion, since Macdonald was Macneil's brother-in-law.

But in November 1625 Father Cornelius Ward arrived in Barra and began what was to become a concerted and successful campaign to bring Barra firmly into the embrace of the Catholic Church. Among his converts were two of Macneil of Barra's sons. Ward was followed by Father Heggarty, who in 1633 claimed to have baptised no fewer than 1,200 of the people in the Western Isles, including Neil Og, the current Macneil himself. A decade later Neil Og was denounced by the Protestant minister on South Uist for keeping a statue of Our Lady in his chapel. Neil Og's response was to invite Father Dermot Duggan to come to Barra to minister to his clansmen, and to support the Stuarts against Oliver Cromwell's roundheads in the English Civil War. Severe Cromwellian laws forbidding the practice of the Catholic faith seem to have been quite simply ignored on Barra, and in 1671 the latest priest claimed his flock numbered more than a thousand. The enthusiasm of the Barra Catholics knew no bounds and in 1675 a Catholic school was opened on the island – only the second such school in the whole of Scotland. Four years later, two Catholic priests were held virtual prisoners by the islanders, who demanded that the clergymen should stay on Barra and minister to their spiritual needs. Barra had clearly become a stronghold of the Catholic faith. Even in 1764, after nearly twenty years of persecution following the collapse of the 1745 Jacobite rebellion, a visitor to the island could find only fifty Protestants among its 1,300 inhabitants.

When the Catholic King James II was deposed in the revolution of 1688, it was hardly surprising therefore that Roderick Dhu Macneil of Barra should take clansmen to support the Earl of Dundee in an attempt to restore a Catholic king to the throne. Dundee raised King James's standard in April 1689, and had assembled a sufficient force by July to meet and defeat a loyalist army

Killiecrankie, where a Jacobite army, including the Macneils, defeated a loyalist force in July 1689.

at Killiecrankie. Macneil and his men fought alongside Dundee, but whereas they survived, Dundee himself was killed. A month later the Jacobite army was beaten at Dunkeld, and further defeats followed. By 1692, the Jacobite rebellion had collapsed and Macneil, along with other highland chiefs, was forced to take an oath of allegiance to King William.

James II never recovered his throne, but when he died in 1701 his son and heir, James Edward, was proclaimed as James III not by some minor Scottish earl but by Europe's most powerful nation, and England's deadly enemy, France. The political, and ultimately the military, support of France gave new credibility to the Jacobite cause. France also gave James Edward a safe haven from which to plot his return to his father's kingdom. In 1708 James Edward set sail from Dunkirk with a force of 6,000 French troops to reclaim the throne. But the invasion fleet was pursued around the British Isles by the Royal Navy and eventually straggled back to Dunkirk having failed to land any troops at all.

The succession of George I, a Hanoverian Protestant, in 1714 encouraged the Jacobites to try again, and the Earl of Mar raised the standard for James Edward on 6 September 1715. He assembled a force of about 8,000 men at Perth, mainly composed of highlanders, among whom was Roderick Dhu (XXXVIII) of Barra and a small force of Macneil clansmen. They flocked to the cause partly to restore a Catholic king to the throne and partly to try and thwart the expanding power of the Campbells, who were firmly allied to the Protestant and Hanoverian cause. Mar sent a smaller force first to Edinburgh, and then to join up with rebel groups in southern Scotland and Northumberland and to invade England. They eventually reached Preston, via Lancaster, but found little support for the cause in the north-west. When Hanoverian forces surrounded the Jacobites at Preston they were forced to surrender on 14 November. James Edward himself had failed to appear in time to rally the highlanders and others to the cause, eventually landing at Peterhead just before Christmas. By this time it was, of course, too late and early in 1716 he returned to France, leaving his supporters to face the music. Roderick Dhu had returned to Barra, but his sons James and Roderick had fled to France to avoid the risk of capture.

After an unsuccessful attempt to repeat the invasion, with Spanish forces, in 1719 the Pretender retired into exile. But the Jacobite cause was far from dead, and when England and France resumed their normal state of enmity, France assembled an invasion fleet of barges to carry 10,000 French soldiers across the Channel for a landfall in Essex and a direct march on London. In February 1744 all was ready, and the English were unprepared, but a huge storm scattered the French fleet and sank or badly damaged many of the invasion barges. Nevertheless, James Edward's son, Charles Edward (Bonnie Prince Charlie), was now ready to pursue the family claim to the thrones of England, Scotland and Ireland.

James Edward Stuart, the 'Old Pretender', who sought to recover his father's throne, in the Jacobite rebellion of 1715. (Courtesy Musée de Versailles)

Right: The Earl of Mar for whom Roderick Dhu Macneil and his men again turned out in support of the Jacobite cause in 1715.

Below: Charles Edward Stuart, 'Bonnie Prince Charlie', in whose 1745 rebellion Macneil of Barra became involved.

Plans were laid for the Young Pretender to land on the west coast of Scotland with 6,000 troops, arms for 10,000 men, and a war chest of 30,000 gold pieces. But when he turned up off the coast of Barra on 22 July, in his French frigate the *Du Teillay*, he was accompanied by just seven companions and, apart from some arms, he had only 4,000 gold pieces to fund his campaign. Many highland chiefs got wind of this underwhelming show of force and declined the invitation to join him. The prince made no attempt to land on Barra, but Macneil's piper joined the ship and piloted it safely to Eriskay, where the prince made his way ashore. He spent his first night on Scottish soil in a humble blackhouse.

A message was now sent to Roderick Dhu's son and successor as Macneil of Barra, known in tradition as Roderick the Dove of the West, suggesting that he should make the short voyage from Castlebay to Eriskay and meet up with the prince and his retinue. The reply came back that, as it happened, Macneil was away from home. There has been much speculation as to whether this was a 'diplomatic' absence, whereby the Macneil was able to postpone making a commitment to the cause. But the prince certainly believed that Macneil was a loyal supporter and a Spanish ship arrived in Barra in October carrying 2,500 stands of arms and $4,000 which Macneil was to hold for the prince's use.

Macneil stored the arms and cash, but inevitably word of the Jacobite cargo got around and on 1 December orders were sent to the prince's representative on Barra, Don Macmahon, to move the arms and the money at once to the prince's comptroller of supplies. Macneil was probably relieved to see it go, and there were signs that he was already wavering in his support for the Young Pretender. The letter conveying the orders to Don Macmahon said that 'if the Laird of Barra does not come out with you with all his kinsmen' then Macmahon should approach Macneil of Vatersay and 'apply to him for assistance'. But Macneil of Vatersay, a mere tacksman, could not be expected to muster much in the way of a military force.

Furthermore in the 1720s he had been much involved with the rabidly anti-Catholic Society for the Propogation of Christian Knowledge. In a desperate attempt to persuade Macneil of Barra to declare himself for the prince, Macmahon was also instructed to tell him that a French army of 6,000 men had now arrived in the south to support the Young Pretender's campaign. In fact, though French support was expected, it had not materialised.

Nevertheless the ploy appears to have worked, for in January Macneil issued a receipt for £10 to Macmahon, specifically 'to bring up my men for his Royal Highness' service'. At the same time Macneil gave Macmahon a promissory note 'to be out with my men to convey Pastich of war for his Royal Highness'.

So now, apparently, the die was cast. Macneil reportedly raised 120 men who were to act as an escort for the arms and money which was to be conveyed to the prince's army. Once the escort had met up with the main force, it seems

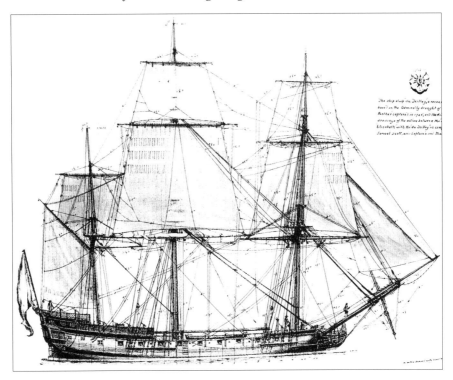

Bonnie Prince Charlie's ship the *Du Teillay*, which picked up Macneil's piper as pilot on 22 July 1745.

The settlement on Eriskay, part of Macneil's territory, where Bonnie Prince Charlie spent his first night ashore in 1745.

unlikely that it would have simply handed over the cash and weapons and then gone home. It was presumably intended for the Barra contingent to become part of the Jacobite army. Preparations for Macneil and his men to go south continued throughout January.

But Macneil's preparations and promises were now an open secret. Macdonald of Sleat, who held the superiority of Barra, tried desperately to intervene on his client's behalf, urging Macdonald of Boisdale to persuade Macneil to hand over the arms and money he still held to save him from disaster. Whether Boisdale made the attempt or Macdonald of Sleat himself warned Barra of the likely consequences of his actions we do not know. But Macneil certainly seems to have had second thoughts about the whole venture, for having made preparations to take his men south, he then remained immobile in Barra throughout February and March. When Bonnie Prince Charlie and his highlanders were defeated at the Battle of Culloden in April, only two Macneils are recorded in the muster rolls of the Jacobite army, they being John and Roger Macneil of Vatersay, enrolled in Clanranald's regiment.

At the beginning of April Macneil handed over £380 left in his safe-keeping to the prince's aides. A few days later on 8 April he was seized by Hanoverian forces led by Captain Ferguson, who reported to the Duke of Cumberland that he had seized Macneil to prevent him from joining the Pretender's forces. Ferguson found three chests of arms, a barrel and a half of gunpowder, two boxes of ball-shot, and some flintlocks hidden away by Macneil, along with $160. Further searches on the island revealed more than a hundred stands of arms that it was alleged Macneil had distributed to his tenants. If these were not evidence enough of Macneil's treachery, the receipt and promissory note that he had signed in January fell into the government's hands in June. Macneil was first questioned by General Campbell, and then hauled off to Inverness to await his fate.

Meanwhile Barra was occupied by several hundred 'Redcoats' under Captain Ferguson's command, partly in the hope of capturing the Bonnie Prince himself, who was now on the run somewhere in the Western Isles. In fact, he was briefly hiding in a cave on the east coast of the neighbouring island of South Uist. But Ferguson's soldiers were also there to hunt down any Jacobite rebels and they seem to have carried out their task with an excess of enthusiasm. A platoon of troops under the command of Captain Scott was sent to Mingulay to arrest the well-known Jacobite sympathiser Father James Grant, but they also seized and summarily executed a local man who, it was claimed, had fought for the Young Pretender. Returning to Barra with Grant, Scott's men arrested and hanged another islander for the same offence. The condemned man, a Protestant, is said to have loudly proclaimed his innocence, to no avail. The Redcoats also seized Donald Macneil of Vatersay's son, Hector, who was dragged off to prison, and subsequently died, probably of typhus. Roger Macneil of Vatersay, who had fought for the Pretender at

General Campbell of Ardmore, who personally interrogated Roderick Macneil of Barra after his arrest in 1745. (Courtesy National Galleries of Scotland)

Culloden, was seized, incarcerated and then transported to the Americas. With such severe punishments being handed out, Macneil of Barra's prospects when he was hauled off to Inverness appeared bleak to the say the least.

At Inverness Macneil and other rebels were herded aboard the prison ship *Pamela* and transported to London. They arrived towards the end of August and were kept aboard the ship for two months, fed on a ration of half a pound of bread and a quarter of a pound of cheese a day. Eventually, at the beginning of November Macneil and some of the other prisoners of consequence were taken off the *Pamela* and placed in the house and custody of William Dick, a government messenger. Macneil remained there until the end of May 1747, when, despite the evidence against him, he was suddenly discharged and allowed to return to Barra. There has been much speculation that he was released as a result of his turning King's Evidence, though no evidence to prove this claim has been produced. It is possible that the efforts of his superior, Macdonald of Sleat, to protect him at last bore fruit. Macdonald of Sleat was regarded by the Hanoverian government as a 'zealous friend' and he may have been able to exert influence in the right places to get the Macneil released.

Returning to Barra, however, Macneil found that the world had changed. Whereas the government had reacted with some restraint after the Jacobite rebellion of 1715, they now enacted laws to crush the Catholic religion and in particular to ensure that the lairds and clan chiefs abandoned the faith. Catholics over the age of fifteen were not allowed to inherit estates, nor could they acquire property either by purchase or gift. Catholic parents had their children taken and given into the care of 'well-affected' (i.e. Protestant) friends or relatives. The parents were required to pay for their children's support from their income or the sale of their property. Under such onerous legislation, the Catholic lairds and chiefs, including Macneil of Barra, had no choice but to give up their faith. Macneil's son, who in clan tradition has come to be called 'Roderick the Resolute', married a Protestant Vatersay Macneil and adopted his wife's faith. Just ten years after his father had been imprisoned as a traitor against King George, Roderick the Resolute swore an oath of allegiance to the king and was gazetted as a lieutenant in the 78th Highland Regiment of Foot. Two years later he laid down his life for King George on the Heights of Abraham during General Wolffe's successful attack on Quebec.

His father, however, may have remained a Jacobite to the end of his life. As late as 1750 a Jacobite spy reported to the exiled Charles Edward Stuart that Macneil was ready to bring a force of 150 Barramen to support a new rising in the highlands. Nothing came of it, and the government, who had got wind of the proposed plot, seem to have left the old man in peace.

For over a century, from the time of the English Civil War, the Macneils of Barra had supported the Stuarts. Initially their enthusiasm for the cause may have been fuelled as much by the hope of arresting the ever-growing power of the Campbells as by restoring a Catholic king to the throne. But Roderick, the Dove of the West, appears to have harboured a genuine commitment to the Jacobite cause, even when that cause seemed lost. In the 1745 he seems to have been torn between his heart and his head, wanting to support the Young Pretender but hesitating to commit himself and his clansmen in the field. In the event, he spent the entire period of the rebellion on Barra, doing enough to implicate himself but little to assist the prince. Given the severity of the punishments handed out by the victorious Hanoverian army under the Duke of Cumberland, he was fortunate to have avoided the confiscation of his estates and prolonged imprisonment. But though he may have continued to harbour sympathy for the Jacobite cause when he returned to Barra, both he and the cause were a spent force. When he died in 1763 Macneil Jacobinism died with him. He was succeeded as chief by his grandson, still a minor, who had been raised a Protestant and who, until he reached adulthood, would be brought up by his uncle, Angus Macneil of Vatersay, a Presbyterian minister. While the vast majority of their clansmen remained devout Catholics, future Macneils of Barra would be firm adherents to the Protestant faith.

7

Gentleman Farmer – Civilising a Highland Chief 1760–1822

By the time Roderick, the Dove of the West, died in 1763 the position and circumstances of the highland clan chiefs had changed dramatically. They had lost much of their independence, first to the kings of Scotland and then to the rulers of the United Kingdom. Initially they were required to attend the Privy Council in Edinburgh once a year, and then to send their heirs to the lowlands for their education. Gradually they were being encouraged to become city dwellers and gentlemen. Following the Jacobite rebellions they were denied the right to wear their kilts, to play their pipes and carry their weapons. At the same time they had been forced to abandon piracy and raiding, which had formerly contributed to both their prestige and their wealth. Perhaps the most symbolic sign of the changed times for the Macneils was that they had abandoned their ancestral and iconic castle stronghold early in the eighteenth century and were now living in Borve township on the west side of the island.

When Roderick the Dove died in 1763 he was succeeded as Macneil of Barra by his grandson, who was only seven or eight years old. The condition of the estate which he inherited can be gathered from the description of Barra by the Reverend John Walker, who visited the island in 1764. According to Walker, the population numbered 1,285 persons, of whom all but fifty were Catholics. They had recently lost twenty-five men (who had followed Roderick the Resolute to death and glory) in Canada, eighty souls to a smallpox epidemic in 1758, and another seventy to a similar epidemic in 1762. The island had also lost much of its best agricultural land following several years of severe storms which had dumped sand over the low-lying fields in Eoligarry at the north end of the island. Macneil's tenants earned enough to pay the chief his rent by making kelp (for which labour the chief paid them) and by selling fish to Glasgow. Their subsistence relied partly on raising a small number of cattle, partly on growing barley, partly on fish and shellfish, and partly on potatoes, which according to Walker had only been introduced to the island in 1752. Farming and fishing were both still carried out in traditional ways with much

The Reverend John Walker, who visited Barra in 1764 and wrote a useful account of what he saw there. (After W. Jardine)

of the land hand-cultivated by the spade, and the fishermen relying on small boats which could only safely fish the nearer bank, a mile off the east coast.

By the time the new chief, who in clan tradition came to be known as Roderick the Gentle, died in 1823 there had been significant changes in many respects, not a few of which were due to the efforts of the chief himself. He was raised from the time of his grandfather's death by his uncle, Angus Macneil, the Protestant minister of Vatersay. At first he was educated on Barra in the school founded by the Society for the Propagation of Christian Knowledge, whose mission was to subvert the Catholic children and hopefully turn them into Protestants. When he was old enough he was sent off to school in Aberdeen – there was not enough money to pay for schooling in Edinburgh or Glasgow – where he may well have encountered the same James Grant who had been imprisoned as a Jacobite in 1746 and was now a Catholic bishop in the city. The Reverend Walker feared that the young Macneil would succumb to the influence of his clansmen and people like Bishop Grant, and forsake his Protestant faith – but he never did. He matriculated at the University of Glasgow in 1769, but there is no evidence that he ever attended this or any other university. Instead he returned to Barra and, under the guidance of his uncle, he learned how to run his estate and be a clan chieftain.

Whether he felt a compulsion to follow in his father's footsteps we do not know, but when another war broke out on the American continent in 1776 – this time with the rebellious colonists – he emulated his father by joining the army and encouraging his clansmen to do the same. In 1778 he joined the Duke of Hamilton's regiment (the 82nd) as lieutenant and in August of that year, sailed to Halifax, Nova Scotia. The following June the regiment was sent to Maine, and thence in 1780 to Charleston and eventually to Yorktown, where on 19 October 1781 along with the rest of General Cornwallis's army, they surrendered to the Americans and became prisoners of war. Eventually in 1783 they were released. At least fifteen of the clansmen who had enlisted with their chief chose to stay in North America, and take up grants of land on the north coast of Nova Scotia. Roderick himself sailed back to Britain and eventually signed off in June 1784.

His five years in America may have been a formative period in his life, for on his return he set about the reorganisation and improvement of his estate with zeal. He began by visiting Europe, particularly the Low Countries, to see how things were done there. Visiting Barra in the 1780s John Buchanan noted that Macneil 'encourages all kinds of improvements', and significant changes can indeed be identified in many aspects of the island's economy between 1780 and 1820.

In agriculture Macneil took the lead by buying good-quality stock from the mainland, rearing a herd which according to the *Statistical Account* of 1794 was the equal of any found in Scotland. He also encouraged the use of the plough, in those limited areas of the island where there was sufficient depth

Cornwallis's surrender at Yorktown in October 1781 saw Roderick the Gentle become a prisoner of war. (Courtesy of the Architect of the Capitol)

of soil and absence of rock to make its use possible. To improve the land and preserve the thin soils from the effects of wind erosion, he drained some of the waterlogged soils in Eoligarry, and planted trees in some areas on the east coast of the island. He was particularly keen to encourage the enclosing of arable land, and offered permanent leases (as opposed to the normal annual ones) to tenants who cleared and enclosed their fields. Although many of the tenants opposed this, it seems to have been at least partially successful, with much of the barley crop now being grown in enclosed fields.

Macneil wanted to go much further than just enclosing arable fields, however. He wanted to create larger farming units than the tiny tenancies occupied by most of his clansmen on Barra. He set the pattern himself by establishing his 'home farm' on the Eoligarry peninsula at the northern end of the island, and created a second farm by taking back into his possession the northern part of Vatersay, centred on Caolis. This had been in the possession of the Vatersay Macneil who was Macneil of Barra's senior tacksman and close relative. Elsewhere, he created five farms on the west side of Barra rented out for nineteen years at a fixed rent, and another at Balnabodach on a seven-year lease.

Whether Macneil was also responsible for improvements in the island's fishing boats and tackle is uncertain, but there was certainly a dramatic increase in the number of fish caught and sent to market in Glasgow between

1764 and 1794. The annual catch of ling had grown five-fold in this period, to 30,000 fish a year, accompanied by a 20 per cent increase in their price. The increased catch at this time seems attributable mainly to a proliferation in the number of boats in operation, from five in 1764 to between twenty or thirty in 1794. Whether or not this was itself encouraged by Macneil establishing new tenancies in some of the east coast areas where there was little or no arable land is unknown, but it was a policy adopted by his son and heir in the 1820s. But by 1816, when the geologist John Macculloch visited Barra, larger boats capable of carrying a dozen men rather than five or six were operating out of Barra, and provided for the first time the opportunity to safely fish on the richer but more exposed outer bank in the Minches. Macculloch notes that the construction of the Barra boats 'is very peculiar' and gives quite a detailed description of them. As their peculiarity perhaps implies, these boats were built by the Barramen themselves with timbers purchased from 'northern traders'. It may well be that Macneil provided the cash to purchase good-quality timbers, and he certainly continued to allow the fishermen to sell their fish directly to the markets in Glasgow, rather than requiring them to sell their catch through him.

The third area of the island's economy which Roderick the Gentle developed with enthusiasm was kelp production. Kelp, a glassy material high in alkali content, acquired by burning seaweed, was used in the manufacture of soap and glass. Its production on Barra began, according to the Reverend Walker, in 1763 – the very year that Roderick became chief. Production on Barra rose from 40 tons in 1763 to 200 tons in 1794, by which time manufacturers in Liverpool were paying £4-10-0 a ton for it. Macneil's enthusiasm for increasing production was therefore understandable, and all the more so with the onset of the Napoleonic Wars. With access to Spanish barilla – a rival source of alkali – cut off, the price of kelp shot up, reaching a peak of around £20 per ton. Macneil benefited twice over from the buoyant kelp market, for in addition to the big increase in income from the sale of kelp, he was also able to raise his tenants' rents because their income had also been increased by the wages he paid them for gathering the seaweed and burning it to produce the kelp.

In the period between 1780 and 1820 there is no doubt that Macneil's income from his estate must have seen a very significant increase. He used his new wealth to fund an increasingly lavish lifestyle. On his home farm at Eoligarry he built a fine Adam-style residence of considerable size and pretension. A two-storey building with a basement and, later, an attic, it was approached by a driveway leading into a flight of seven steps. The front door was flanked by four stone pilasters, and gave onto a large entrance hall. To one side was the drawing room and to the other a dining room and pantry. An impressive staircase provided access to the four first-floor bedrooms and bathroom. The basement housed a kitchen, pantry and domestic stores, and

The walled garden and farmyard of Barra House, built by Roderick the Gentle, seen here *c.* 1940 towards the end of its life. (Comunn Eachdraidh Bharraigh agus Bhatarsaigh)

a laundry room. A servants' wing built onto the rear of the house housed five bedrooms and two further storerooms. Further outbuildings included a ten-stall stable, two loose boxes, a bull house, a nine-stalled byre, and two sheds for calves. Surrounding the entire complex was a 3-metre-high wall which enclosed an acre of garden where fruit and vegetables were grown.

To service Macneil's needs Barra House was staffed with a cook, a housekeeper, a maid, a kitchen maid, and a groom. The home farm employed about twenty people including a gardener and dairy maid, as well as herders and agricultural labourers. This might have been an excessive staff for a single man, but in 1788 Roderick had married Jean Cameron of Fassifern, and a couple of years later celebrated the birth of a son and heir, inevitably christened Roderick. Six further children followed, all but one of which were girls, so that by about 1805 all four bedrooms at Barra House were fully occupied.

At the time of his marriage, his father-in-law had described Roderick Macneil as 'a very genteel young man'. While one cannot imagine any of his predecessors as chiefs of the Clan Macneil being so described, it is a description of which Roderick himself would almost certainly have approved. To mark his new-found status as a forward-looking landlord and gentleman, Roderick employed the famous portrait painter Henry Raeburn to produce portraits of himself and his wife. Roderick is shown in a three-quarter-length green coat with a black velvet collar and a white jabot. He wears buff breaches and holds a large, floppy hat in one hand and a hunting gun in the other. Standing in a

Barra House, the Adam-style mansion built at Eoligarry by Roderick the Gentle *c.* 1790. (Crown Copyright, RCAHMS)

hilly, lightly wooded landscape, he looks both nonchalant and confident – a man who is comfortable with his place in society.

Initially at least, the two portraits were presumably hung in the dining room of Barra House, but later they may have been moved to Roderick's other residence in Liverpool. With the kelp industry looming ever more important in the profitability of his estate, Roderick began to spend more time in Glasgow and Liverpool, where the bulk of his kelp was sold. By 1810 he was listed in the local Liverpool directory as a resident of Brownlow Street, and his occupation was given as 'gentleman'. In 1814 he was similarly listed living at Mount Vernon Street. His neighbours in both streets were mostly merchants. Around 1816 he moved house to the then semi-rural Toxteth Park. Letters sent by him to the parish priest of Barra from this time onwards were written in spring, summer, autumn and winter so that he appears to have spent most of the year in Liverpool. Although he still had siblings living in Barra House, his links with the island and its people were becoming ever weaker.

In fact the relationship between the Macneil of Barra and his kinsmen had been deteriorating for decades. Some time before 1776, he had built a mill at Northbay to which his tenants were forced to send their corn for grinding, for which service they were charged. To make sure they used the mill, their own hand querns were confiscated. The establishment of the west coast farms around 1775 saw tenants ejected from an area of better land and either given

Roderick the Gentle, painted by Sir Henry Raeburn *c.* 1790. (After Sotheby's)

new plots created in more marginal areas or forced to become agricultural labourers on the new farms. When the home farm was established at Eoligarry in the 1780s, the existing tenants lost their plots, although they were given new ones elsewhere on the island. None of this would have endeared him to his kinsmen.

But the changes he implemented in the period from 1790 to 1820 seriously exacerbated the situation. The rapid expansion of kelp production between 1790 and 1815 was not without its costs to Macneil's tenants. Not only did he require them to undertake the hard and unpleasant task of harvesting the sea wood, standing waist deep in the cold waters around the coast of Barra for hours on end, but he forbade them to any longer collect sea wood to manure their lazy beds on which they grew their potato crop. Furthermore, the kelping season fell in the summer and they were forced to spend their time at the kelp just when they most needed to spend it looking after their crops and animals.

At the same time some tenants saw their plots subdivided. The population of Barra rose between 1764 and 1811 from 1,300 to 2,100, and together with the creation of the home farms and the west coast farms, this put an intolerable strain on the availability of land on which to create new plots. While some new plots were laid out in areas previously thought too poorly provided with cultivable land to be viable, others were created by dividing existing plots in half. Although the creation of these new plots may have been undertaken with good intentions, they undoubtedly also suited the Macneil very well. He had more tenants, paying more rent, who were forced to work on the kelping because their land was too poor or too small to otherwise support them. But inevitably it bred discontent among the tenants.

Nor did smaller plots or plots in marginal areas mean that the tenants were paying lower rents. Between 1794 and 1811 rents in Barra rose over 300 per cent. This was, of course, exactly the period in which the price of kelp rose sharply and kelp production became increasingly important. Because the tenants were being paid for their labour at kelping, they were judged to be capable of paying increased rent for their plots of land. Much of the cash they earned from their kelping they never saw because it was simply retained by the Macneil to pay their (increased) rents. Finally, his determination to see much of the land enclosed seems to have met with stiff resistance from at least some of his tenants. He refers to the issue several times in his letters to the parish priest and in 1818 wrote, 'I will use every exertion, that the land and the hay are permanently divided: those for and against it will show me, who I must look to and who not.'

There were thus good reasons why Macneil's kinsmen should have become increasingly disillusioned with their chief who, in the traditional relationship between chief and kinsmen, was expected to look after their welfare. Yet both contemporary commentators and later clan tradition claim that Roderick the Gentle still strove to be the protector of his people. The Reverend Buchanan in 1790 said the Macneil 'exercises justice among his tenants, and protects them from those oppressions which are too common in other parts of the Hebrides'. The Reverend Macqueen in 1794 records how Roderick gave money, land, and new agricultural tools, to a group of former tenants who returned destitute from the lowlands of Scotland. He reports too that in bad years, when the crops failed, Macneil imported corn from the mainland which he sold on to his tenants at cost. Even in the manufacture of kelp he showed a willingness to share his good fortune by paying his tenants £2-12-0 a ton for the kelp they produced, which was said to be the best wages paid anywhere in the Western Isles. And when smallpox broke out in 1800, perhaps recalling the two lethal epidemics of his childhood in 1758 and 1762, he immediately brought in a doctor and arranged for the inoculation of his tenants.

Certainly Roderick himself, in his surviving letters to Angus Macdonald the parish priest, claims to still accept his responsibilities not just as a landlord but as a chief. In June 1816 he speaks of 'the people to whom I am so much attached', whom he is 'more ready to serve for love', and in August he reminds the priest that 'I have at all times been willing to come forward for the protection of the people of Barra'. When he lost 300 of them to emigration in 1817 he seemed genuinely distressed: 'the loss of so many very decent people is much to be regretted ... when one reflects he has seen for the last time those he has been accustomed to from early infancy'. Even after his move to Toxteth Park he still talks of coming 'home' to Barra. Even that scourge of the 'improving' landlord, John Lorne Campbell, concluded that Roderick the Gentle was 'a chief of the old type, warmly attached to his tenants and his property'.

Be that as it may, there is no doubt that by the end of his life, Roderick had become increasingly alienated from his kinsmen. Putting aside resentments caused by raised rents, restrictions on the use of kelp as manure, the removal of tenants from good lands to poor, and the increasing enclosure of lands, Roderick had gradually erected barriers between himself and his people.

One was physical – his own removal initially from Borve, living among his clansmen, to the northern peninsula of Eoligarry, from which tenants were now excluded, and then from Barra altogether as he became a city-dweller in Liverpool. The second was symbolic – his construction of Barra House, a fashionable home more suited to the city than the highlands and islands, and alien to Barra in style, design, materials, and in the society which lived in it. It was a visual and enduring statement that the Macneil of Barra was now more a gentleman than a highland chief.

Thirdly the spiritual barrier which had existed between the Protestant child and his overwhelmingly Catholic kinsmen had gradually grown higher through the years. Roderick had provided a new schoolhouse for the Society for the Propagation of Christian Knowledge, whose mission, in addition to providing an education for the island's children, was to undermine the

Catholic faith. His attitude to his Catholic kinsmen was said to have become increasingly 'arbitrary and despotic' and in March 1790 things came to a head. Roderick, having refused permission for the building of a new Catholic church, came upon four of his Catholic tenants discussing a possible location for the banned building. A furious argument ensued as a result of which the entire Catholic population of the island – about 1,600 souls – threatened to emigrate. In the event the majority stayed put, but twenty-eight families (perhaps around 150 people) sailed for Prince Edward Island on the *Queen of Greenock* in 1790, and there appears to have been a further exodus of about 200 people to British North America two years later. Macneil and the Catholics fell out again in 1799, two letters from the parish priest at this time referring to 'Barra's persecution' and saying that his 'conduct from first to last has been of a more black complexion than I at first imagined'. It may be that this particular episode led directly to a further significant emigration of tenants, to Nova Scotia, in 1801 and 1802. He lost over 600 more tenants to emigration in 1817 and 1821, although these were probably motivated more by a combination of favourable economic circumstances than any sense of religious persecution.

Barra in 1820 was probably more prosperous than it had been when he became chief in 1763, but it was overpopulated, despite the series of emigrations. Furthermore its modest prosperity was precariously balanced. It depended heavily on the continued demand for kelp, and its population depended just as heavily on the potato as their principal source of sustenance. When Roderick the Gentle died in April 1822, at his home in Toxteth, he left behind him discontented tenants and, despite the economic boom of the Napoleonic era, a mountain of personal debt.

8

Emigrants – Leaving Barra
1770–1840

The fifty years of Roderick the Gentle's chiefdom between 1770 and 1820 coincided with a significant increase in the number of people emigrating from the highlands and islands of Scotland. Some of these went to the lowlands of Scotland, where the growing needs of industry created a constant demand for new sources of labour. One such group left Barra, for example, around 1790 to work in David Dale's cotton factory in Glasgow. But many of the emigrants left Scotland altogether and crossed the Atlantic to settle in British North America (or Canada as it became in 1867). Although the emigrants from Barra made up only a small part of the total number of 'highlanders' who made this journey, Barra gave up perhaps as high a proportion of its people to transatlantic emigration as any part of the highlands and islands. Barra's population in 1770 was around 1,300 people and in 1820 about 2,000. It is estimated that over this period of time about 3,000 emigrated from Barra to North America.

The flow of emigrants, however, was by no means a smooth, continuous process. Rather it saw a series of short episodes when hundreds left the island in the space of just one or two years, separated by long periods when there were few if any emigrants. It has been noticed that this ebb and flow in the emigrant tide reflects the beginning and end of a series of wars. At times of war the flow was drastically reduced; in times of peace emigration increased significantly. Thus in the period between the end of the Seven Years' War in 1763 and the outbreak of the American Revolutionary War in 1776, between the end of that war in 1783 and the beginning of the wars with France in 1793, between the Treaty of Amiens in 1802 and the renewal of war with France in 1803, and finally following the defeat of Napoleon at Waterloo in 1815, there were sudden peaks of emigration. In each of those peaks, the people of Barra played a part.

The first group emigration took place in 1772, when eight Barra families were induced to join a party led by John Macdonald of Glenaladale.

Macdonald was a Catholic tacksman on South Uist, where Colin Macdonald of Boisdale had been threatening his Catholic tenants with expulsion if they did not abandon their faith. Supported by the Catholic Church, Glenaladale managed to purchase 20,000 acres of land on the Isle of St John (later known as Prince Edward Island or PEI) in the Gulf of St Lawrence. In order to get the 200 emigrants he needed to make the venture viable, Glenaladale recruited families not only from South Uist, but also from the mainland, from the tiny island of Eigg, and from Barra. The spokesman for the Barra contingent was a carpenter called Allan Mackinnon, and he and his companions (being unable to write) duly put their 'mark' against their names on the tenancy agreement which they were given when they landed in PEI on 24 June 1772. I was privileged to see and read this document, which survives in the archives of PEI, in 1998, and what a remarkable document it is. Mackinnon and his fellow emigrants, who were used to holding plots of no more than 2–4 acres of poor-quality land on a lease which the landlord renewed, or not, every year, can scarcely have believed their good fortune. They were offered plots of 150 acres of good arable and grazing land towards the west end of PEI on a lease which would run for no less than 'three thousand full and complete years'.

This emigration was clearly sponsored and instigated by the Catholic Church, who did so primarily to warn Boisdale of the consequences of his attack on the Catholic faith of his tenants. On Barra, Glenaladale seems to have found a willing accomplice in Father Alexander Macdonald, the parish priest in 1770. But whether the Barra emigrants themselves joined the party for religious reasons is by no means certain. At this time there is no evidence that Roderick the Gentle was persecuting his Catholic tenants. And a second document lying in the archives of PEI suggests that perhaps the motivation for emigration was more economic and social than religious. Within just three months of signing their 'dream' tenancy agreement, the Barra families as a group paid a penalty and left their plots, because they wanted to find and purchase their own freehold lands. Quite simply, however good the terms of their tenancies, they wanted nothing more to do with landlords and the powers they exercised over their lives.

A second, much larger, group emigration took place from Barra in 1790, followed by a further one in 1792. On this occasion the emigration was organised by a professional emigration agent, Simon Fraser. When the *Queen of Greenock* left Tobermory in July 1790, twenty-eight Barra families (probably between 100 and 150 people) were on board. After suffering at the hands of a series of severe storms, the ship finally docked at Charlottetown, PEI, in September. In 1792, by which time the Barra families were settled on land at Grand Rivers, a second emigrant ship, again organised by agent Fraser, arrived in PEI with up to 200 people from Barra on board. They in turn settled in Indian River. For Barra to lose over 300 of its people – one in six – in just two years must have been traumatic, and one inevitably wonders what drove so many to leave the island at this time. A period of peace may have facilitated emigration, but it can hardly have caused it on this scale. The only known event on Barra itself which seems relevant is Macneil's outburst of fury at his Catholic tenants' determination to build a new church in the face of his opposition. We may recall that the entire Catholic population of the island (more than 90 per cent of its total) are said to have threatened to emigrate over this matter. The emigrations to PEI in 1790 and 1792 suggest that a significant number of them chose to do just that.

A brief lull in the wars with revolutionary France saw another outburst of emigration fever on Barra in 1801 and 1802, but two apparently large group emigrations in these successive years are both something of a mystery. Two ships, the *Sarah* and the *Dove,* were involved in 1801. When they sailed from Fort William, they carried a total of 569 men, women and children. A complete list of the names and place of origin of every one of these passengers survives; not one of them is from Barra. Yet there is a persistent tradition that after leaving Fort William the ships took on additional emigrants – from Barra.

There may be some support for this contention from two opposing sources. The Highland Society was trying to prevent emigration from the highland estates, and they claimed that the ships actually carried 700 passengers, rather than 569. It was said that a third tier of bunks had been built into the *Sarah* and hidden behind a partition. The emigration agent responsible for organising the voyage, Hugh Denoon, also claimed, some nine years later, that his ships carried 700 emigrants to Nova Scotia in 1801. Oral tradition on Barra later in the nineteenth century said that when Barra men enquired

Hugh Denoon, of Pictou, Nova Scotia, who organised a controversial and somewhat mysterious emigration of an unknown number of Barra people in 1801.

about a passage on the two ships there were not enough places left, and some were disappointed, but others were taken on. There is perhaps one way in which the discrepancies might be resolved. Hugh Denoon had very cleverly persuaded the customs authorities that it was not fair to count children as full passengers. It was agreed that the ages of all children under the age of 16 be added together and then divided by 16 to arrive at a notional number of full passengers represented by the children. In this way the notional figure of passengers on the two ships was recorded not as 569 but as 426. If Denoon had indeed managed to smuggle an extra 130 or so Barra emigrants on board after the ship left Fort William, then he would have had an actual complement of about 700, but a notional total of about 570. So we believe that perhaps up to 130 Barra people took part in the emigration of 1801. Surprisingly, however, we know the names of only two of them.

These two men were both the sons of Macneil tacksmen, Roderick Og Macneil of Brevig, and James Macneil of the neighbouring township of Earsary. Their purpose in taking ship in 1801 seems to have been to spy out the land, and make their own arrangements for a second substantial emigration in 1802. James Macneil returned to Barra in 1802 to organise the emigrant families, but unfortunately drowned in an accident in the Minches. His brother Hector Ban Macneil took on the task and successfully carried over a large party of emigrants to Nova Scotia, including Roderick Og's father and family. A report on emigration from the islands in 1802, written at the end of that year, claims that 600 (or perhaps even 1,000) people left Barra that year. These figures seem excessively high, but a report written in 1806 says that 900 emigrants left Barra and the Uists in 1802 in two unnamed ships. Although the details are unclear, it seems that there was indeed a significant emigration in 1802. This is confirmed in a variety of documents including land petitions, and we have identified more than fifty Barra families who claimed to have emigrated in 1802.

The final mystery concerning the emigrations of 1801 and 1802 is what encouraged so many families to leave their ancestral homeland and sail to Canada at this particular point in time. There is a little evidence that Roderick the Gentle was again at odds with his Catholic tenants in 1799/1800, but not enough to suggest that it stimulated their migration in these numbers. Poor harvests in 1801/02 may have encouraged small tenants to think about emigration, although the continued surge in kelp production offered an alternative source of support. The lull in hostilities with France may have provided a window of opportunity for safer voyages and low fares but this alone is unlikely to have stirred up any serious outbreak of emigration fever. Equally, the arrival of Hugh Denoon in the Hebrides early in 1801 and his vigorous campaign to recruit emigrants may also have been fortuitous but would not of itself explain the sudden surge of so many Barra people to cross the Atlantic.

1. A small rock shelter near Allt Easdal, which excavation showed had been used in the Neolithic, perhaps as a good place from which to hunt seals and seabirds in the waters immediately below.

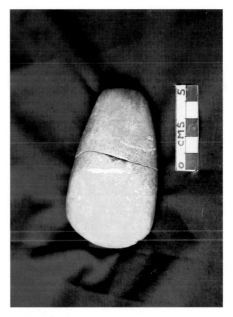

Above left: 2. A complete beaker found in the storage box on the back of the stone hut at Allt Easdal, with fine impressed decoration.

Above right: 3. A polished stone axe-head from the early Neolithic occupation of Allt Easdal *c.* 3000 BC.

4. The unusual 'paved' cairn above Allt Easdal which contained a burial cist approached down a narrow central passage.

5. A low cairn of cobbles and burnt beach pebbles covering the pyre remains at the centre of the cairn VS4B.

Above: 6. The top half of a 'standing stone' partly overlain by the revetment of the inner cairn, and subsequently completely buried within the cairn.

Right: 7. Fragments of a bronze cloak-fastener probably dropped by a mourner during the building of the kerbed cairn at VS4B.

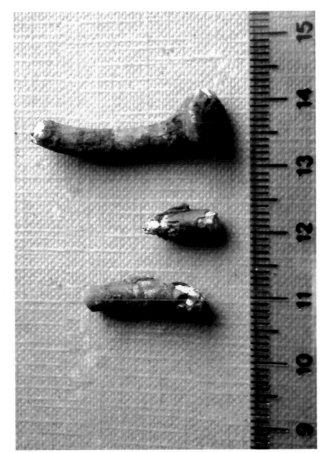

Above: 8. A broch tower with a well-preserved wall elevation at Dun Dornaigil, Sutherland; its tiny doorway can be seen at the far right. (David Brinn)

Below: 9. The wall of a broch on Borve headland, incorporated into the modern cemetery wall, with a doorway still visible.

Right: 10. Students recording a newly discovered wheelhouse high above Castlebay.

Below: 11. The prominent position on a headland, occupied by the broch of Dun Ruadh, Pabbay.

12. A standing stone on Borve headland, a spot chosen by Norsemen to bury one of their wealthy women.

13. Kisimul Castle, ancestral home of the Macneils. The upstanding masonry outside the curtain wall to the left is all that remains of the galley house.

14. Holyrood Palace, Edinburgh, where Rory the Tartar was questioned by King James.

15. The early Christian cemetery and chapels at Cille Bharra.

Right: 16. The surviving gable end of Macneil's mill at Northbay, to which all his tenants were required to take their corn to be ground.

Below: 17. Toxteth Park, Liverpool, where Roderick the Gentle died in April 1822.

18. The tenancy agreement between John Macdonald and eight Barramen for plots of land on Prince Edward Island, 1772. (Courtesy Public Archives of PEI)

19. Vernon River, PEI, where Roderick Og Macneil of Brevig, Barra, settled with his family in 1802.

Above: 20. The Macdonald house of *c.* 1830, the home of an emigrant family, now preserved in the Highland Village at Iona, Cape Breton. Note the two storeys and the many windows.

Below: 21. The north wall of Macneil's chemical factory at Northbay with its double-gated portals (now blocked) set straight into ships at high tide for loading products.

22. The market cross in
Edinburgh at which Roderick
Macneil was publicly declared
'His Majesty's rebel'.

23. The 78th Highlanders in
1842 when Roderick Macneil
was appointed to command
them in India.

24. Hyde Park Gardens, London, where General Macneil lived the last years of his life.

25. The townships of Borve (nearer) and Craigston. Craigston was cleared of crofters and turned into a farm by Colonel Gordon in 1840.

26. The foundations of two adjacent blackhouses perched on the edge of the east coast in Bruernish, surrounded by barren land and rock.

27. The site of Balnabodach on the shore of Loch Obe, cleared by Colonel Gordon in 1851 but soon reoccupied.

28. Houses built after Gordon's clearance at Balnabodach.

29. The sandy beach of Bagh Siar (West Bay), Vatersay, on which the victims from the *Annie Jane* were washed ashore. The ship had hit the headland in the background and broken into three pieces.

30. The estate house on Vatersay where some of the survivors from the *Annie Jane* were housed following the disaster.

31. The deserted village of Mingulay from which the last families had moved to Vatersay, Sandray and Barra. The red-roofed building in the distance is the chapel. (P. Foster)

32. The site of Sheader on Sandray where five of the households from Mingulay initially settled before being evicted. The mound on which they built their houses proved to have a long sequence of occupation beginning in the Bronze Age.

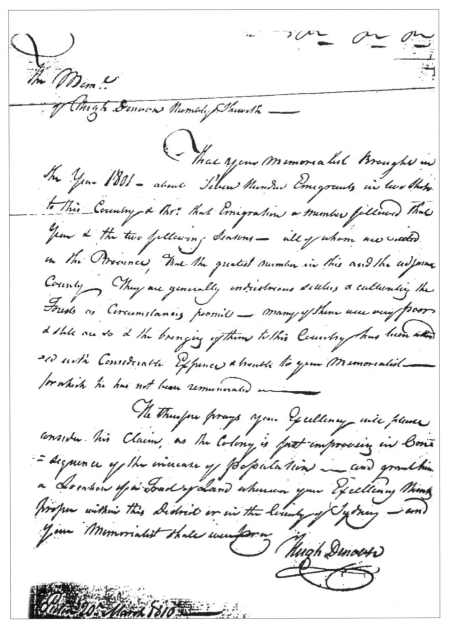

A petition by Denoon in 1810, referring to his emigration party in 1801. (Courtesy of Public Archives of Nova Scotia)

A promissory note for £3-5-0 from John Macneil to emigration agent Simon Fraser, being the balance of his passage on the *Hope* in 1817.

The remaining unknown factor in the equation is the role of the two Macneil tacksmen from Brevig and Earsary, whose sons seem to have been key figures in organising the 1802 emigration. Many tacksmen throughout the island estates had become increasingly unhappy with their lot. Their income from the sub-tenants who occupied some of their enlarged plots had been eroded as the landlords had increasingly taken some of this land back to rent out directly to tenants themselves. In 1801/02 the Highland Society noted that many of the emigrant groups in those years were being led and organised by disillusioned tacksmen. Denoon had himself used two such Clanranald tacksmen from South Uist as recruiting agents in 1801. It may be that they in turn had encouraged their fellow tacksmen from neighbouring Barra to stir up emigration fever there and had been responsible for ensuring that Roderick Og and James Macneil had secured two of the scarce spare places on board the *Sarah*. Certainly these two tacksmen earned a place in Barra tradition as the instigators of the emigration of 1802.

In 1803 the renewal of hostilities with Napoleonic France and the passing of the Passenger Act, which trebled the cost of a transatlantic passage overnight, led to an immediate cooling of emigration fever. On Barra it was not to break out again until Napoleon had been defeated at Waterloo in June 1815. Then, in a letter to Angus Macdonald the parish priest in June 1816, Roderick wrote from Liverpool, 'Reports have of late come to me of a spirit of emigration from your parish: but having no hint from you on the subject I paid little attention to them. Matters, however, are now so far settled; a considerable number having signed with a Mister Fraser.' This was apparently the same Simon Fraser who had organised the emigrations of 1790 and 1792, with the assistance of Bishop Macdonald, after Macneil's opposition to the building of a new Catholic chapel. In 1816, if Roderick had heard about the planned emigration from Barra in Liverpool, then the parish priest would certainly have known all about it – but he had apparently not mentioned it in his correspondence with Macneil. In two further letters that summer Macneil never once opposes the emigration, but rather offers his best services to try and get better terms – a cheaper fare and better provisions – for his departing tenants. But his tenants apparently rebuffed his offers of help and did so with some vehemence. In a letter of August 1816 Roderick wrote, 'I confess I am hurt that any man in Barra should want confidence in me, much more think me capable of abusing their confidence.'

In May 1817 two ships, the *William Tell* and the *Hope*, sailed from Greenock with a total of 382 emigrants on board. The vast majority of these passengers were reported to have come from Barra, and most of them disembarked at Sydney at the north end of Cape Breton in July. Records kept by Governor Ainslie of Cape Breton confirm that Roderick the Gentle's fears about Simon Fraser's promises concerning provisions for the emigrants were well founded. In a letter to the Colonial Office he complained, 'I possess no means to afford them the supplies of provisions with which Mr Fraser deceived them with hope of, and for giving them the implements of agriculture they expect. They have been much deceived.' Altogether we think about 300 Barra people were involved in this emigration, and we can trace in the various records of the time the names of about 200 of them. Almost all of them settled around the Bras d'Or Lake in the centre of Cape Breton which had become a magnet for Barra emigrants from 1800 onwards.

Surviving receipts reveal that the Cape Breton authorities not only provided some provisions and tools for the emigrants in 1817 but also paid for their transport by boat from Sydney to the southern end of the Bras d'Or. In fact records in Britain and Cape Breton reveal that the government were involved in assisting this emigration from the beginning, offering help with provisions and ordering the customs and exercise to exempt the emigrants from any duty payable on items they were taking with them. Why this exceptional help was offered to this particular group is unknown, but government letters put it down to 'the particular circumstances' in which the Barra people were placed at this time. But what were these circumstances? We have no idea – there is no suggestion of a bad harvest or food shortages in 1816–17. Nor is there any suggestion of a further falling out between Macneil and his Catholic tenants. Indeed in his letter of June 1816 Macneil tells the priest that 'in the building a chapel, I will with pleasure accede to what you think' – a very different reaction to that of 1790. The only clue is to be found in a letter

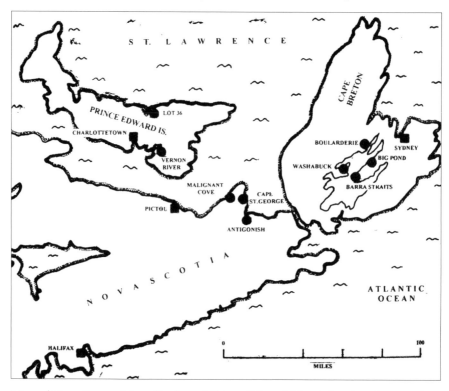

Map of Cape Breton, Nova Scotia and Prince Edward Island showing the ports into which Barra people sailed and some of the main places where they settled.

from the Undersecretary to the Colonies in April 1817 which implies that the 'circumstances' are explained in the enclosed letter from Mr Fraser. Sadly Simon Fraser's letter does not survive, but it seems that he managed to spin a good enough tale to win a quite exceptional degree of government support for his little venture.

At the time of the 1817 emigration it appears Simon Fraser had plans for a further group to follow in 1818, but in the event the next group emigration did not occur until 1821, when the *Harmony* left Barra for Sydney, Cape Breton, with 350 passengers. There is no reason to think that they were all drawn from Barra itself, but we know the names of about 150 Barra people who claimed to have arrived in Cape Breton in 1821 and were presumably on the *Harmony*. This was the last emigration from Barra to be witnessed by Roderick the Gentle before he died in 1822. Altogether he had seen seven group emigrations during his chiefdom, and an ongoing trickle of small groups and single families which, though less well documented, contributed significantly to the outflow. Between 1770 and 1820 Roderick probably lost about 3,000 of his tenants and kinsmen. Although he may have been partly culpable in stimulating the departure of some of them, the Catholic Church and priests, the tacksmen, and the emigration agents also had their irons in the fires of emigration fever.

Roderick's heir and the new chief of Clan Macneil took a very different view of emigration, and indeed of his tenants and kinsmen. Roderick Macneil, the forty-first chief of the clan, was in his mid-thirties when his father died. At the time he was a major in the Life Guards, and he attempted to run his estate from London and Windsor, making only brief visits to Barra. He tried to woo the parish priest with fine words and some personal favours, but the wily Angus Macdonald had an agenda far removed from that of the Macneil. Although matters only came to a head in 1826, it seems that Macdonald had been stoking the fires of emigration from a much earlier date, working both with Simon Fraser and local agents Macmillan and Macniven. His role in the emigration of 1826 was plainly recognised both by his successor on Barra and by the priest of neighbouring South Uist. Writing to Macdonald in 1826 after he had left Barra, Father Chisholm of South Uist says that the people are 'on the wing to emigrate if they possibly can. The ferment you left, and perhaps fermented among them, has not as I find in the least abated.'

When news of plans for an emigration first reached the Macneil in London in February 1825 he let the parish priest know very clearly what his reaction was. 'I have little dread of emigration. I certainly shall in all the various ways in my power (and they are not a few) oppose it.' By July he had come to the conclusion that he could not in fact prevent his tenants leaving, but he ordered Macdonald to read his 'proclamation' in church as soon as he received it. After laying down the law to his kelpers and fishermen, the proclamation turned to the emigrants. 'Say to those who are about to emigrate that I sincerely wish them well through it' – and then the sting in the tail – 'and assure those who have signed and repented that their repentance comes too late – So help me God, they shall go, at all events off my property, man, woman, and child.'

And go they did, though not until 1826 and 1827. There are no detailed records which tell us how many left Barra in these years, but in June 1826 400–500 people from Barra and Uist had applied for a passage, and the Bishop of PEI wrote to Macdonald in December of that year saying 'many of your flock from Barra came to Cape Breton this last season'. A smaller number followed in 1827. Although individual families continued to leave through the 1830s this was the last of the documented group emigrations under the Macneils. The new chief, who had threatened in any case to expel some of his tenants and replace them with Protestants, did just that and brought in people from the Uists, Tiree, Skye and to a lesser extent the mainland. We can identify forty to fifty of these immigrant families on Barra in the 1830s and 1840s.

For many years the emigrations from the highlands and islands between 1770 and 1840 were seen as the result of pressure from the landlords to clear their property so it could be leased out more profitably to lowland

The entrance to Pictou harbour, still surrounded by dense pine forest even today.

tenants, especially for sheep-grazing. That was undoubtedly true of some areas, particularly on the mainland. But elsewhere, and particularly on Barra, there was no such pressure. And certainly from about 1790 to 1820 Macneil preferred to keep his tenants, who provided his kelping labour force. The emigrations from Barra between 1770 and 1840 were undertaken by people who chose to seek a new and better life in North America, though certainly encouraged to do so by the Catholic Church and the emigration agents, and at times by discontented tacksmen.

Initially many of the emigrants found life hard in Cape Breton and Nova Scotia. Barra's climate, though windy and exposed, is known for its generally mild winters, very different to the winters experienced around the mouth of the St Lawrence and in Cape Breton. The forests, which offered some protection from the worst weather and endless supplies of wood for fires were, nevertheless, the bane of the emigrants' lives. For people coming from a treeless landscape the dense and all-pervading forests were dark, threatening and claustrophobic. Clearing them for even small cultivation plots was a back-breaking task and one for which Barra men were of course totally unprepared. As a result many emigrants had to spend valuable cash buying the services of a logger. There was too the sense of both physical and cultural isolation. In a small island like Barra everyone knew everyone else, and indeed lived within a few miles of them; in Cape Breton, 160 times the size of Barra,

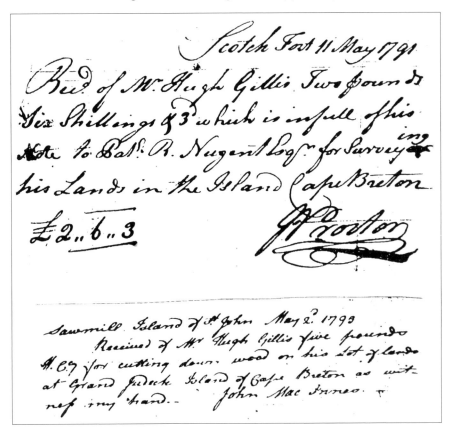

Receipts for fees paid for surveying and clearing a plot of land in Cape Breton. (Courtesy PANS)

the population was very thinly spread. And that population was made up of people of very varied origins – native American, French, Irish, English and Scottish – speaking different languages and with very different patterns of social behaviour and material culture.

But there were compensations. Cape Breton provided far better farmland than Barra, was well populated with deer and other wild animals, and had both sea-coasts and the great Bras d'Or Lake which were rich in fish. Above all, land grants were generous – at least 100 acres and often much more – and most important of all to Barramen, they were made 'for ever' to the applicant and his heirs. Within a few decades, many of the Barra immigrants were boasting flocks, herds, and grain harvests beyond their wildest dreams in Barra. Roderick Og Macneil, for example, settled at Vernon River, PEI, and in the census of 1841 is recorded as owning two horses, fourteen cattle, twelve sheep and ten pigs, and producing 325 bushels of oats and 450 bushels of potatoes, as well as smaller quantities of wheat and barley. Furthermore, by this time he had become an elected representative to the PEI Legislative

Assembly – a pillar of the local community. Roderick Og's descendents still live on the same plot of land to this day.

With the income they earned from the sale of their surplus produce the Barra emigrants bought all sorts of little luxuries. In time, they were also able to invest in fine timber houses with two floors, plenty of windows, and separate bedrooms, dining room, and kitchen, in other words houses which were very different from the Barra blackhouses. A fine example built in about 1830 is preserved in the Highland Village at Iona in Cape Breton.

Such prosperity and the occupation of houses with five or six separate rooms threatened to sweep away the very basis of the society in which the emigrants had grown up. But their firm adherence to their Catholic religion and their Gaelic language prevented this from happening. They soon built new chapels, and there and in the home they spoke only Gaelic. Family histories, island stories, and Gaelic ballads continued to be recited and sung around the fire on long winter evenings. The names they gave to natural features, to locations, and to their own plots perpetuated and recreated the memories of Barra. Around the Bras d'Or you could soon find Barra Straits and Barra Head, visit Castlebay, Borve, Kilbar and Craigston, and gaze at MacKinnon's Harbour, Gillis Lake, Macdougal's Point, and Macneil's Beach. Even today, there are hundreds of families in Cape Breton, Nova Scotia and PEI whose roots lie in Barra and who keep alive the tales and memories of that tiny island 3,000 miles away on the other side of the Atlantic.

9

The General –
The Last of the Ancestral Line
1790–1863

The last chief of the Clan Macneil to bid farewell to his emigrating clansmen was Roderick Macneil, forty-first chief, known in clan history as The General. He was the first son of Roderick the Gentle and was born around 1790. His childhood was spent at Barra House, surrounded by five younger sisters and a much younger brother, Ewan. By the time he was seventeen he had decided where his future career lay, and he told his maternal grandfather that he wanted to be a soldier: 'I think that an intelligent and skilful officer in the army is as respectable a character as any.'

In pursuing an ensignship, he could present a respectable family tradition in the military. His grandfather had fought and died at Quebec, his father had fought in the American War of Independence and was now colonel of the 10th Inverness Militia, and his maternal uncle, John Cameron, was already making a name for himself in the British Army. But the key to Roderick's pursuit of a commission was his father's friendship with one of Britain's most successful generals. During the American War of Independence, Roderick the Gentle had served alongside a young Lieutenant John Moore. John Moore was now General Sir John Moore, who as commander of the 52nd Oxford and Bucks Regiment had introduced a rigorous new training regime which was to make the British light infantry the envy of Europe. In March 1808 Roderick the Gentle wrote to Moore seeking his help. Moore immediately responded, writing a personal letter to the Duke of York, commander in chief, recommending 'the name of Mr Roderick Macneil for one of the vacant ensignies in the 52nd Regiment'. 'He is a young man of a proper age,' wrote Moore, 'and the son of a Highland Chieftain, an old friend of mine and formerly in a regiment with me in America.' Within forty-eight hours, Roderick received a commission as ensign in the 52nd. Furthermore, when father and son travelled south to meet General Moore in April, Roderick the Gentle was able to tell his father-in-law that 'General Moore … was so good as to take particular charge of Rory, assuring me that he would be sure to see he came on'. There was clearly the prospect of a successful career, and perhaps accelerated promotion.

Sir John Moore, eminent soldier, friend of Roderick the Gentle, and patron of his son. (Ian Fletcher)

Roderick Macneil's regiment the 52nd Light Infantry on the march in Iberia in 1808. (Ian Fletcher)

The young ensign went off to Shorncliffe in Kent for an intensive introduction to the particular skills of the light infantry. He learnt drill, how to use firearms, how to skirmish, and how to drill a company of soldiers. He received his uniform – red jacket, buff breeches, cross-belts, black 'shako', and his sword – and was promised the sum of £160 per annum for his service. He barely had time to appreciate all this, and complete his training, before his regiment received orders to prepare to go to war. He wrote to his grandfather on 3 July to tell him that he was awaiting embarkation, and by the time he finished the letter he could add a postscript – 'our destination is supposed to be Cadiz'.

With the French driving back Spanish armies in Iberia, the government had decided to send assistance to Britain's allies. Two divisions were sent to Portugal, and the 52nd were in that commanded by General Anstruther, which landed – in difficult conditions and with some loss of life – at Paymayo in mid-August. Within two days of landing Roderick had his first experience of war when the British division defeated the French at Vimiero. Shortly after, Sir John Moore was given command of the British forces in Iberia and after reorganising and strengthening his army he marched into Spain at the end of October. But further Spanish defeats and the arrival of Napoleon himself to command the 170,000 French troops in the peninsula forced Moore to begin a retreat towards the port of Corunna in the north-western tip of Iberia. Sensing the opportunity to smash the British Army, Napoleon undertook a vigorous pursuit of Moore. Roderick found that his regiment was selected to form part of the rearguard which had the unenviable task of fighting off the French cavalry which were attempting to reach the main body of Moore's army.

For four weeks in the depths of the Iberian winter, Roderick and his colleagues spent day after day desperately repelling the French, and then hastily retreating to the next defensible position. The route to Corunna wound slowly upwards through the bleak Cantabrian mountains. It was freezing cold, the snow lay deep, and the army and its camp followers were rapidly running out of rations. The wounded, the starving and the freezing were dropping and dying along the roadside, and discipline was breaking down. At Cacabellos Roderick witnessed his first floggings, as the rearguard's Commanding Officer, Edward Paget, punished looters with 800 lashes. Shortly after, a fierce close-quarters engagement with the French cavalry left the road 'choked with their dead'. By the time Roderick eventually reached Corunna he had been initiated into the full horrors of early nineteenth-century warfare. Eventually, on 16 January 1809 the British troops embarked in the waiting transports. But not before a final pitched battle with the French, in which Roderick was wounded and his patron, Sir John Moore, was killed.

While Roderick was convalescing from his wounds he heard that he had been promoted to lieutenant. By July he was fit and back in uniform and joined 40,000 troops sent on the Walcheren expedition in the estuary of the River Scheldt. Flushing was quickly captured and little more than 100 British troops died in action. But a deadly fever took hold and, over the next few months, 4,000 died and 11,000 were laid low, most of whom were eventually invalided out of the army. Roderick appears to have survived unscathed, and after returning to Britain he transferred to the 91st Argyll Highlanders in July 1810. Eventually, in 1813, he was once again sent to the Continent, landing in western Pomerania and then undertaking a long march through the autumn and the winter to Flanders. The following March his battalion were part of the force which attacked the fortified town of Bergen-op-Zoom. Three-quarters of the 4,000 British troops involved were killed, wounded or taken prisoner – but again Roderick appears to have led a charmed existence. In December 1814 he purchased a captaincy in the 60th Loyal American Regiment, one of the largest regiments in the army with eight battalions, which were spread around the globe. His father provided the £2,000 purchase price.

But this was simply a career move. Within forty days he had found a captaincy in a new regiment – the 23rd Light Dragoons. Roderick had been riding since at least the age of seventeen, and we must assume he had become at least a competent horseman to take up this post. For him it had obvious attractions – a 40 per cent pay increase, and rather dashing uniform, and the opening up of new possibilities for advancement in one of the prestigious cavalry regiments. His transfer went through in January 1815.

An officer of the Light Dragoons, in which Roderick Macneil became a captain in January 1815. (Ian Fletcher)

Five weeks later Napoleon escaped from Elba, and within three weeks he was back in power, in Paris, and raising a huge army. In early April the alarmed British government sent nearly 20,000 troops to swell Wellington's small army. Among them were Roderick and the 23rd Dragoons. When Napoleon advanced on Belgium in June, the 23rd were hastily moved to join the force that was to intercept them at Quatre Bras. When the French advance units clashed with the British there on 17 June the 23rd Dragoons did not distinguish themselves, but they were nevertheless ordered to form part of the rearguard to slow down Napoleon's advance. After retreating north that evening Roderick and his fellow dragoons were onlookers in the early stages of the Battle of Waterloo the next day, but in the later afternoon were active protecting British infantry squares, pursuing French cavalry, and taking part in the final advance of the British across the battlefield.

Roderick returned to England at the end of the 1815 and remained on active service and full pay, although in 1817 his father reported that his son 'has been dangerously ill ... and is now at Cheltenham in a convalescent state'. In 1818 he married Isabella Brownlow, daughter of Baron Brownlow of Lurgan, Armagh, a man of considerable wealth. After visiting the Continent, Roderick returned in 1819 to purchase (with his father's money) a commission as captain in the prestigious 1st Life Guards. He briefly transferred to the 84th Foot in 1821 in order to obtain promotion to major, but after four months returned, as major, to the Life Guards.

How much he kept in touch with, or was interested in, the affairs of his father's estate in Barra is unknown, but there is certainly no evidence that after leaving Barra in 1808 he had set foot on the island again in the following fourteen years. He had spent that time sporadically taking part in some of the bloodiest and most desperate battles of the time, escaping relatively unscathed from all of them, while skilfully negotiating a series of promotions. In 1822 Roderick could look back on his military career to date with some satisfaction, and look forward to the future with some expectation. But then his father died, and Roderick inherited both his father's estate and his role as the chief of the Clan Macneil.

The problems facing both the estate and Roderick were immense. To begin with, his father left debts to the tune of about £30,000 (the equivalent of over £2 million today), while establishing annuities to the value of almost £1,000 per annum for Roderick's sisters, and offering a lump-sum settlement of £5,000 to his younger brother Ewan. Roderick also discovered that in 1820 his father had taken out a Deed of Probate which meant that on his death the management of the estate was entrusted to twelve trustees, and quite explicitly denied Roderick any say in its running. Roderick the Gentle seems to have thought his eldest son either too committed to the army or too incompetent to run the estate. Certainly the new Macneil had no experience of managing farming, fishing or kelping and had so far shown little interest in the island's affairs. Roderick also had to face the fact that he had lost 200 of his tenants to emigration only twelve months before his father's death, and perhaps more than 500 in the previous five years. That meant the loss of perhaps a hundred rents, and rather more pairs of hands to help cut and process kelp. Finally, Roderick's succession to the chiefdom of Clan Macneil coincided with the beginning of a steep decline in the demand for and market price of kelp. This was due partly to a series of duty reductions on seven raw materials which were involved in providing alternative sources of alkali, but most of all to the introduction of the 'Leblanc' process for converting salt into alkali.

While lawyers spent the next four years wrangling over the Deed of Probate, Roderick tried to get to grips with the declining economic situation. He decided that his tenants must work harder and used a carrot-and-stick approach to persuade them to do so. He sent provisions, new fishing tackle, and tools and materials to employ people improving the roads and trackways on the island. But he also insisted that they had fewer holidays, that fishermen sold their catch through him and that rent arrears were to be paid in full. He threatened to evict those who would not comply – 'they shall never again eat a potato on my property' – and said he would replace them with Protestant tenants. The latter threat was aimed at the Catholic Church, and its embodiment on Barra, the priest Angus Macdonald, but recognising the 'unbounded influence' which Macdonald had over his flock, Roderick also offered personal inducements as well as compliments to the priest.

But neither the priest nor the tenants were inclined to respond positively to the Macneil's exhortations, and relations between chief and kinsmen rapidly declined even further. In 1825 Macneil appointed a new factor to run the estate. This was Alexander Stewart, who became a close friend of the most notorious of all highland 'clearers', Patrick Sellar, and shared his hard-nosed views as to how to make highland estates profitable. Stewart devised a simple plan for Barra: 'My plan ... was to remove hordes of small tenantry from the west to the east side so as to get at the most valuable of the pasture for stock and to put down fishing settlements on the south and east.' Macneil accepted the plan and in July 1825 sent Angus Macdonald what he called a 'Proclamation' which the priest was to read out to his flock at Sunday service. It took an uncompromising line to kelpers, fishermen and would-be emigrants, and threatened any who did not follow the instructions of Mr Stewart to the letter with immediate eviction and exile.

Stewart set about collecting rent arrears, with Roderick 'determined that every penny of rent would be paid at the term'. Those who could not pay had their livestock seized. Meanwhile Macneil had begun to establish a fishing village at Castlebay and was actively seeking recruits with experience of deep-sea fishing among the fishermen of north-eastern Scotland. The rest of the fishermen would come from the tenants cleared from the west coast townships. Between 1828 and 1836 new crofts were created on small and generally barren plots of land on the east coast, most notably around the Bruernish peninsula. Evictions on the west coast were begun in 1826/27, and the priest who replaced Angus Macdonald in 1826 wrote to his predecessor the following October saying that Stewart had unroofed all the houses in Borve, Tangusdale and Allasdale that summer. Removing or burning the roofs of tenant's houses was found to be an effective way of forcing them to leave their homes. But the same letter also said that Stewart had left Barra, and Stewart himself told Patrick Sellar that Macneil did not have the perseverance to see the process through. It may be that the mass emigrations of 1826 and 1827 had unnerved Roderick.

In any event, with Stewart leaving, west coast clearances in abeyance, and the fishermen still not performing to Macneil's satisfaction, Roderick's attempts to turn around the economic fortunes of his estate looked doomed to failure. It was at this point that he met a 'Welsh chemist' who claimed to have a process that would dramatically increase the alkali content of made kelp. Both the name of the chemist and the details of his process were and remain a mystery, but Roderick was convinced by the Welshman and took the momentous decision to build a factory at Northbay to carry out the re-processing of kelp. He purchased bricks for the building of its chimneys and furnaces in 1828, and by March 1830 the works were said to be complete. At Northbay you can still see the 3-metre-high outer wall of the factory enclosing an area almost 40 metres square. Although the buildings inside have long since been demolished, we know they included various workshops and a 'mixing house, carbonating furnace room, and a crystallising house' where the essential part of the process was carried out.

The ambitious scale of the work is indicated above all by the seven double portals set in its seaward wall, and the low-water jetty built at its north-west corner. These were clearly intended to allow large quantities of kelp, made kelp and re-processed kelp to be moved into and out of the factory at both high and low tide. It was said that Macneil employed 500 people in the manufacture of kelp, but this figure presumably includes the crofters who cut and burnt seaweed as well as those working in the factory. The labour force in the factory itself may have come from Mingulay and Berneray, since a report by Robert Stephenson in 1838 said that Macneil had cleared these islands and forced the tenants to work at the Northbay factory. Given both the scale and the nature of the venture, it is fair to claim that Roderick Macneil introduced the industrial revolution to Barra.

However, the factory only slowly built up towards full production, and it was five years after its completion before that stage was reached. Meanwhile Roderick was getting desperate and he began to pursue unpaid rents with new vigour. In 1831 he himself led his factor and ground officers across the island seizing cattle from those tenants in arrears. He had already moved north from London to Helensburgh on the Firth of Clyde and so that he could personally oversee both the chemical factory and the running of the estate he now took up residence at Barra House. There he employed seven domestic servants, as well as eighteen farm workers, and continued to live in some style.

But the debts which his father had left had now been dwarfed by those taken out to fund the building of the chemical works. Between 1829 and 1833 he borrowed about £55,000, over half of it from a Liverpool entrepreneur, Harold Littledale. His creditors were pressing for payment, and although the chemical works were now producing an annual profit possibly as high as £1,500, it was too little too late. In September 1836 one of his minor creditors, Colonel John Gordon of Cluny, demanded his money back and Roderick couldn't or wouldn't pay. On 28 September a royal Messenger at Arms proceeded to

Harold Littledale, whose loans financed Macneil's chemical factory. (After *The Daily Post* 1889)

the Market Cross in Edinburgh and loudly denounced Lieutenant Colonel Roderick Macneil as 'His Majesty's rebel'. A warrant was issued for the arrest and imprisonment of Macneil, but when the law finally tracked him down to his temporary lodgings in Edinburgh he had, not surprisingly, absconded.

Roderick had returned to Barra, where he quickly set about making arrangements to save what he could of his personal belongings from the clutches of his creditors. And they proved to be many and varied. As a gentleman he was expected to owe money to his tailor, bootmaker, grocer and wine merchant, and other assorted tradesmen. But substantial as these sums were, they were tiny compared to the accumulated debts owed to various investors and companies. When the final tally was made by the trustees appointed to administer the sequestered estate, it came to more than £115,000 – the equivalent of something approaching £8 million in today's money.

The trustees set about the task of selling off his assets, such as they were. They sent their appointed agent and factor, Charles Shaw, to Barra as the long Hebridean winter was setting in. His task was to make an inventory of the furnishings of Barra House and the chemical factory, and to similarly do a stocktaking of the estate and its livestock. On arriving in Barra, he went straight to Barra House, where he was confronted by an irate Macneil who, having berated him for arriving unannounced, told him to come back in ten days' time. Shaw said that was not practicable at that time of year, at which Roderick sat him down and proceeded to discuss the history and affairs of the estate in considerable detail. In fact he kept Shaw occupied for more than two hours, at the end of which Roderick said it would be fine for Shaw to start work the next day.

But as Shaw was leaving the house someone whispered in his ear that, at that very moment, fifty-five of Macneil's prize cattle were being shipped aboard a boat by Michael Maceachern of Arisaig. When Shaw demanded that Macneil stop the shipment, Roderick claimed the cattle had been sold to Maceachern long before, and then broke into a long bluster. By the time he had finished, the boat had sailed. And so it went on. Over the following days Macneil shifted sheep and cattle around ahead of Shaw to try and prevent them being counted, and tried to hide several crates of personal belongings first in the factory and then in a nearby blackhouse. It later transpired that over seventy crates of personal effects, plus a considerable quantity of furniture had already been sent to Maceachern, which explained why Shaw's inventory of the contents of Barra House revealed nothing of value at all. Eventually Maceachern's property was searched and all Roderick's effects were seized and sold off by auction.

The trustees, having heard of all this from Shaw, demanded that Macneil should appear before them for an interrogation. After managing to delay as long as possible, Roderick eventually presented himself at the trustees' office in India Street, Edinburgh, in March 1837. A transcript of this meeting survives and it reveals a wonderful display of verbal swordsmanship as Lieutenant Colonel Macneil parried the thrusting questions of the Edinburgh lawyer Charles Murray Barstow. According to Roderick he had done everything to protect the interests of his creditors, he had certainly disposed of nothing since his estate had been sequestered, and he had made no attempt to hide anything. Barstow eventually gave up trying to wring an admission of guilt from Macneil, but continued to make enquiries, particularly about an alleged missing set of silver plate.

Roderick never returned to Barra, and there is no reason to think he ever gave it or his tenants and kinsmen another thought. He had in truth come to loathe them long before. In his letters to Angus Macdonald in 1825 he spoke of their 'fickleness, idleness, and stiff-necked prejudice ... their inveterate sloth and pig-headedness'. For their part, the people of Barra must have been glad to see him go. He had moved many of them from crofts on good land to new ones on bare and rocky coasts, raised rents, forced many to work in his chemical factory, seized their livestock, and brought in significant numbers of Protestant 'outsiders'. The final tenuous links between chief and clansmen had finally been completely broken.

Roderick took flight to Ireland to stay with his wife's family to avoid the trustees' further attentions and until the considerable opprobrium his behaviour had aroused could die down. He may have had a friend in the War Office, for they had rebuffed attempts by the trustees to raid his half-pay and in 1836 he had been promoted to the army rank of full colonel. In 1841 Roderick took the first step to revive his military career and took a regimental appointment as lieutenant colonel of the 91st Argylls. But nine months later he had still not actually joined his regiment, and was being recorded as 'absent without leave'. He was probably loath to risk being sent to St Helena, where half his regiment were stationed. In the nick of time he managed to transfer to the 78th Highlanders on 15 April 1842. Six days later he, Mrs Macneil and their daughter Caroline sailed with some of the regiment for India!

He served there for thirteen years, first in Poona and Bombay, eventually commanding a division which took part in the invasion of Sind under Sir Charles Napier. In 1848 he was appointed to command the Centre Division of the Madras army, a force of perhaps 20,000 men. There was little military action there at this time, but Roderick managed to get himself appointed to staff duties and just as he was due to return to the 78th at Bombay he was appointed to the General Staff in Madras. He stayed there until the end of 1854, being promoted to lieutenant general and receiving a Distinguished Service Award. He left India in 1855, just two years before the outbreak of the Indian Mutiny, in which his old regiment the 78th were to win eight Victoria Crosses.

During his service in India, Roderick would have had the opportunity to accumulate a modest fortune with which he could hope to live in some

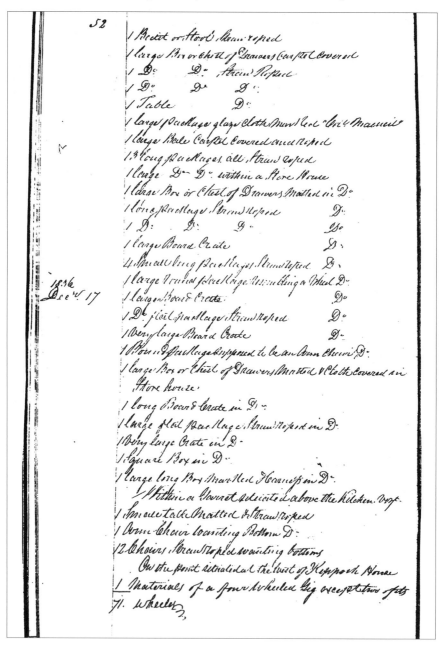

Part of the list of personal belongings of Roderick Macneil found by the sheriff, hidden in a barn at Arisaig. (Courtesy National Archives of Scotland)

General Roderick Macneil *c.* 1860 at the age of sixty-nine. (Courtesy Museum of Queen's Own Highlanders)

comfort in England. His return was marred, however, by the death of his wife, Isabella, at Southampton, shortly after their arrival. Roderick settled in London in an apartment on Bond Street and joined the United Services Club. Out of the blue, in 1858, he married Eliza Middleton, a wealthy widow. He moved into her spacious town house in Hyde Park Gardens. In 1860 he was appointed colonel of his last regiment, the 78th Highlanders, and it was now that his portrait was painted. Two years later he was finally made a full general. Roderick Macneil of Barra was now a fully fledged officer and a gentleman.

On the morning of 22 October 1863 he died, while shaving, at his home in Hyde Park Gardens, at the age of seventy-two. His widow buried him alongside his first wife in a fine mausoleum in the corner of Southampton Old Cemetery. Visitors to the cemetery today can still read Eliza's eulogy inscribed on the side of the mausoleum: 'He was noble in character, exemplary in every relation of life. A gallant soldier, a warm and generous friend and affectionate husband. The last chief of the ancient line.'

The mausoleum where General Macneil and his first wife, Isabella, were buried in Southampton Old Cemetery. (Geoff Watts)

10

The Entrepreneur –
Clearing Barra 1840–1852

When Roderick Macneil left Barra for the last time in March 1837 the forthcoming auction of his ancestral estate had already been announced in the *North British Advertiser*. If the battle of wits between Macneil and the trustees had descended into near farce, then the auction of the Macneil estate proved to be no different. At the auction of 19 April, with a reserve price of £65,000 (£20,000 below Macneil's valuation), not a single bid was received. Within a week the trustees had placed a second advert, in the *Edinburgh Advertiser*, with a new auction date of 24 May, and a reduced reserve of £60,000.

But on 5 May the trustees were thrown into panic when a second advert appeared, in the same newspaper, submitted by one J. J. Fraser, who said that he held the title deeds to the estate! Furthermore J. J. Fraser Esq. had written to the trustees to tell them that their auction was illegal. At this point one of Macneil's minor creditors, Colonel John Gordon of Cluny, produced a conveyance to show that he was now the legal holder of Fraser's heritable bond, and that Fraser had no claim at all on the estate. So the trustees were able to press ahead with the second auction, but with the same result. A third attempt in October was equally fruitless, and in March 1838 the trustees reduced the reserve to just £45,000. A fourth auction was scheduled for October but never took place, and attempts to sell it by 'private bargain' came to nothing. In January 1839, the by-now-desperate trustees agreed to reduce the reserve to a mere £36,000 and to set an auction date in March.

On 6 March, in the coffee house of the Royal Exchange in Edinburgh, the estate of Barra came up for auction for the fourth time. An opening bid of £36,000 was submitted by Captain Duguid, acting for Colonel Gordon. New bids were made by a Mr Warrington of Surrey, and a Mr Menzies (solicitor) of Edinburgh. Duguid offered £40,200, to which Warrington replied with a bid of £42,000, only to be outbid by Menzies at £42,050. At this point the half-hour sandglass ran out, and Mr Menzies was declared the winner. Menzies paid a deposit of £100 but thirty days later had still not provided any security against the outstanding sum. Enquiries then revealed that Menzies was not in fact a solicitor, but simply a solicitor's clerk. His employer was none other than J. J. Fraser Esq. The trustees thereupon offered the estate to the next highest bidder, and Mr Warrington sent a cheque, drawn on the Metropolitan Bank, for £10,000 as his first down payment. But when the cheque was presented the Metropolitan Bank said they had never heard of Mr Warrington and held not a sixpence of his money.

And so, at last, the estate was offered to the third bidder, Colonel John Gordon, at his last bid of £40,200. But Gordon responded that as both of the other bidders had proved fraudulent he should get the estate at his opening bid of £36,000. There followed a series of threats of legal action – from the trustees against Gordon, from Gordon against the trustees, and even from J. J. Fraser Esq. against the trustees (no one could claim that Fraser was not a trier). Eventually on 16 December the estate of Barra was purchased by Colonel Gordon at the price of £38,050. The legal niceties were not completed until the summer of 1841.

By this time, even the crofters of Barra must have had some inkling as to just who had bought the land they farmed. Colonel John Gordon of Cluny was an entrepreneur from Aberdeenshire, whose family had accumulated, over the space of three generations, vast estates in north-east Scotland. The family was noted for their hard-headed attitude to business (and its business was the management of estates), and for their extremely parsimonious attitude to

The Royal Exchange, Edinburgh, where the Macneil estate was finally sold in 1839. The entrance to the Coffee House where the auction took place is at the left.

life in general. Of Gordon's grandfather it was said that 'every shilling he got within his fingers stuck to them', while his father 'declined moving about for fear of incurring expense, and latterly refused even to get up out of bed, on the ground that he could not afford it'. In the Colonel this dislike of unnecessary spending revealed itself by the great detours he took in order to avoid ever paying to use a toll road.

But when it came to business, Gordon was not averse to spending a fortune if he thought that in due course he would get a very healthy return on his outlay. The bankrupt lairds of the Western Isles offered new opportunities to expand his interests in north Britain. He first acquired a financial interest in Barra in 1832 when he bought part of Macneil's debt as represented by the heritable bond held by J. J. Fraser. In 1835 – eighteen months before Macneil went into sequestration – he had a memorandum drawn up on the estate and its affairs. In September 1836 it was he who initiated the final collapse of the Macneil estate by demanding payment of the debt he had purchased from Fraser. In August 1837 he entered into a correspondence with a Mr Macmillan, who had heard that Gordon had visited the island and intended to buy it. Macmillan offered him advice on the quality of the sheep grazing and proffered the opinion that it would be best if the majority of the tenants were shipped off to America. It is hard to escape the conclusion that Gordon had his eye on Barra for some years, but was prepared to bide his time until conditions were favourable to make a bid.

In 1838 he purchased the Clanranald estate of South Uist and Benbecula, and finally declared his hand on Barra in March 1839. Altogether between 1838 and 1850 he spent upwards of £160,000 acquiring and investing in the estates of Clanranald and the Macneils. Despite his later well-earned notoriety as one of the most fervent 'clearers', in 1840 Gordon's reputation as a landlord suggested no great cause for concern. He exercised close personal control of the management of his estates with a firm hand but it was said that 'he liked to have about him the old tenantry, seldom parting with any who had occupied his land for any considerable time'. Two years after he purchased Barra it was reported that he wished to keep all of his new tenants. He also spent considerable sums in his first years of ownership repairing and extending roads, draining waterlogged land, and clearing drifting sand from some of the agricultural land which had recently been engulfed by it. In this way he improved the estate while providing paid work for some of the islanders.

Nevertheless he seems to have followed the same strategy as that proposed in 1825 by Alexander Stewart, by replacing the crofters on the west coast with larger farms, presumably given over to sheep. In 1837 the townships of Craigston. Allasdale, Greian and Cleat had seventy-one crofters; in the 1841 census not one of the heads of family in these townships is described as a crofter – instead there are sixty-five 'agricultural labourers' and seven craftsmen. The majority of the labourers are the same men as had been crofters four years

earlier. In other words these tenants had been deprived of their crofts and had
little choice but to become employees of the farmers who replaced them or to
move elsewhere if crofts were available.

Gordon originally planned to create new crofts in the centre of the island
for displaced tenants from the west coast, but the centre of the island was (and
to this day remains) empty of crofts for the simple reason that it is almost
entirely composed of rock and peat bog. Instead, those former crofters who
did not find or take employment on the farms were provided with new crofts
on the east coast (again, an echo of Stewart's plan for Barra). More blackhouses appeared around the bleak and unproductive coast of Bruernish, and
at Ruleos where between 1841 and 1851 the population trebled. The new
houses at Ruleos, an area unusually short of stone for Barra, were built almost
entirely of turf. When we surveyed the area in 1998 we were able to identify
the last traces of these ephemeral dwellings in which people lived for a decade
or more.

The people settled on new crofts on the east coast between 1825 and 1845
had become almost totally dependent on the potato for their subsistence. They
had too little grazing and that of poor quality to raise much livestock and no
land suitable for other crops. Apart from any fish they caught, they depended
almost entirely on the potatoes they could grow on small lazy bed plots,
which they placed wherever they could find any soil between the bare rock

Potatoes growing on lazy beds – a crop and method of cultivation which precariously
maintained a population of up to 2,000 people on Barra.

and the blanket peat. In 1846 disaster struck the Western Isles as it was hit by the potato blight which had already devastated Ireland. Literally overnight families saw their precious potato crops turn rotten.

Reports of the dire situation in the Western Isles began to appear in the national press, and before long Gordon was being singled out as having done nothing to relieve the distress in which his tenants found themselves. In December 1846 the government sent him a strongly worded letter insisting that he take action. Gordon sent a bombastic reply which was a mixture of anger, irritation and protestations of innocence. Early the following year, however, there had been two deaths on Barra due to starvation, and there was a devastating eyewitness account of the death of a crofter whose only remaining food supply was a single turnip. Pressure mounted on Gordon and reluctantly he responded. By June 1847 the government was able to report that Gordon had sent considerable sums of money and supplies of food to Barra, and had remitted rent arrears. But, as the blight persisted, there came further harrowing eyewitness accounts of near starvation on Barra. A visitor in August described how, when he reached the great beach at Triagh Mhor, 'the whole population of the country seemed to be met, gathering the precious cockles ... starvation on many faces'.

With no end to the potato famine in sight, Gordon took the decision to get rid of a large part of the 'redundant population' which were now a drain on his pocket. In 1848 he began by sending the first shipload of 270 tenants from South Uist to Quebec, and 150 people from Barra to Glasgow, where Gordon paid for temporary accommodation and offered them a passage to North America. The pace of clearance increased in 1849 with nearly 1,000 Uist people shipped abroad. In 1850 it was Barra's turn again, and 132 families (about 600 people) were removed, and sent first to Tobermory and from there to Glasgow, Edinburgh and Inverness. Their pitiful condition when they arrived in the cities aroused great indignation. One Glasgow worthy who wrote to Gordon asking him what he intended to do for his displaced tenants got a swift and Scrooge-like reply, appropriately published in the *Scotsman* on Christmas Day 1850: 'What do I propose doing with them? – I say – nothing.' Gordon said that over the last three years Barra had cost him almost £2,000, he had already sent a cargo of corn to feed the starving people, and he would do no more. He then denied that the people had been turned out on his orders and that 'they must have left Barra of their own free will'.

Impervious to public criticism Gordon now planned the biggest clearance of all for 1851. Five ships were chartered to take over 1,700 of his tenants and their families from Uist and Barra to Quebec. The Barra contingent, numbering almost 450 souls, was ordered to go to Lochboisdale on South Uist; failure to turn up would incur a fine of £2. Mr Fleming, Gordon's factor responsible for overseeing the transportation of these people, wrote to the chief immigration officer in Quebec on 9 August informing him that the *Admiral*, on which the

A nineteenth-century depiction of a classic clearance – the factor and his officers watching the roof of a blackhouse burning while the evicted family walk away with only what they can carry.

Barra people would sail, would leave in a few days. Colonel Gordon, he said, had not only paid their fares and provided food and water for the voyage, but had also given them clothing and shoes. The *Admiral* duly sailed on 11 August and arrived on 1 October.

When it arrived, the immigration authorities were handed a petition signed by Hector Lamont (of Brevig) and seventy of his fellow passengers, which described some of the scenes preceding embarkation, and also the promises they had been made which induced them to 'proceed voluntarily to embark on board the *Admiral*'. These included not only a free passage, but free conveyance on arrival to Upper Canada, the provision of work, and the offer of land grants.

In due course, most of these promises were met, but at the time the immigration authorities in Quebec, having received Fleming's letter, were somewhat shocked to find that the passengers on the *Admiral* were not only penniless and without possessions, but also 'they were in rags ... and destitute of clothing'. In fact the wife of the *Admiral*'s captain said she had spent most of the voyage making whatever clothes she could for them from old bread bags, blankets and bits of canvas. It turned out that the clothes donated by Gordon had been subsequently taken back by his agent, who thought the passengers 'sufficiently clothed'.

As for the lack of possessions, that was apparently part and parcel of the ruthless way in which Gordon's men had removed people from their

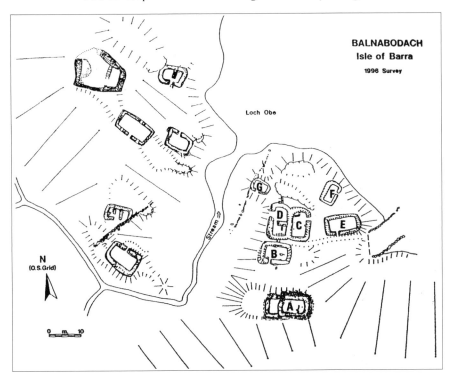

A plan of the settlement at Balnabodach with the houses cleared by Gordon to the east of the stream and the reoccupation houses to the west.

homes. Once people were out of their blackhouses the buildings were made uninhabitable, and it was said that even the temporary tents of blankets the evicted people erected for shelter while awaiting transportation were pulled down. Some passengers had decided not to board ship at Lochboisdale and had been hunted down, sometimes with dogs, and forcibly dragged on board. Meanwhile, Gordon's agent had sent a boat and men to Northbay on Barra to track down and forcibly remove other tenants who had refused to go to Lochboisdale.

Contemporary records and oral tradition on Barra recount some of these events in early August 1851. Jonathan Maclean, a thirty-eight-year-old cottar (landless tenant) living in Bruernish, was finally tracked down and caught on the rocky shore of Ardveenish, and Margaret Macnash, a forty-year-old widow living a little further north at Vaslain, was carried off in the middle of cooking her dinner. From the hill overlooking Vaslain, the daughters of the elderly John Macdougall hid and watched as the people, including their father, were taken off for transportation. At Balnabodach on Loch Obe, sixteen-year-old Michael Maclean escaped removal by hiding on a ledge on a nearby cliff, but a young girl from the same township was seized as she milked a cow and taken away with the just the clothes she stood up in. Some of these events were recorded by John Macpherson (known as the Coddy). John was born in 1876 and as a young man listened to the eyewitness accounts of John Macdougall's daughters, and of Farquhar Macrae, who as a twenty-four-year-old in 1851 had been aboard the *Admiral*.

The events at Balnabodach have a particular interest for me. I first examined the abandoned blackhouses of Balnabodach in 1996 and I was struck by its beautiful location on the loch side. It was such a sleepily peaceful location that the students working with me immediately renamed it 'Brigadoon' (after the imaginary Scottish village in the Hollywood musical that came to life only once every hundred years). While we were making a record of the buildings I got into conversation with a tall, quietly spoken man who came across the meadows to see us. He turned out to be the Coddy's son, Niall Macpherson, and with his enthusiastic encouragement we undertook a much more detailed study of Loch Obe and particularly of Bolnabodach in the summers of 1999 and 2000.

While we revealed traces of both Neolithic and Iron Age settlement beneath the later houses, our particular focus of interest was of course in the houses which we believed to have been cleared by Gordon in 1851. We excavated three of these and in all three the latest dateable pottery was made in 1840–1850, so abandonment in 1850 is likely although it cannot be proven. The excavations revealed that the families who were cleared in 1851 lived with few material comforts. There was no trace of floor coverings of any sort and no remains of 'bed-boxes' built against the walls. The pottery the families used was mostly cheap and cheerful 'sponged wares', though occasionally

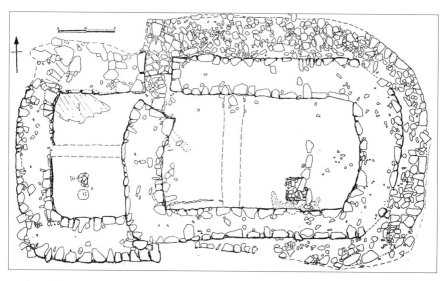

A plan of one of the cleared houses after excavation. The slab-lined hearth is at the east end. The house may have been occupied by Hector Macdugald, his wife, three children and older sister Flory.

a few more colourful items were acquired and one or two family heirloom pieces dating back to around 1770 survived into the middle of the nineteenth century. A few scraps of clay pipes offered little evidence to support the comment of the Revd Buchanan in 1793 that the Barramen were 'extremely addicted to tobacco' – perhaps by the 1840s they could not afford it any more. Apart from fragments of pottery two of the houses produced no material remains at all, while the third yielded only a thimble (lost between cracks in the rough paving outside the front door) two small beads, two buttons, and one or two bronze pieces which might have been fittings on a small box. Given the dark interior of the blackhouses and their earthen floors, one might have expected more from houses occupied for ten to twenty years, even if most belongings were taken away by the occupants. The impression is that the people removed from Balnabodach by Gordon in 1851 had few material comforts.

Altogether Gordon cleared about 1,200 people from Barra. Initially in 1848 and 1850 they came from the west coast townships, particularly of Allasdale, Grian and Cleat, and from some of the offshore islands like Hellisay and Gigha. In 1851 it was the turn of the east coast townships like Bruernish, Ruleos, Balnabodach, Brevig and Glen. But the removed people came from all parts of Barra and its southern islands and the clearance was particularly aimed of course at the landless cottars and those with rent arrears. Gordon's clearance net swept widely and cruelly and there was scarcely a family on Barra that was not affected by it.

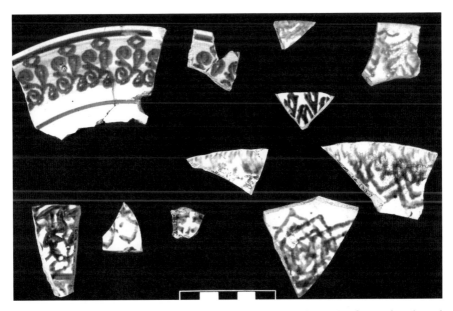

Fragments of cheap and cheerful 'sponge ware' pottery from the floor of a cleared blackhouse at Balnabodach.

11

Lost Souls –
Shipwrecked on Vatersay 1853

The 1,200 people removed from Barra by Gordon of Cluny, having been evicted from their homes and tiny plots of land, had little choice but to accept what was on offer to them – a free passage, modest provisions for the voyage, and the uncertain promises of jobs and perhaps a plot of land. They left Barra in a mixture of desperation, fear, and perhaps a faint hope that somehow things would get better. In every respect they were very different to the passengers who boarded the fine new brig the *Annie Jane* at Liverpool in August 1853, almost exactly two years to the day after the *Admiral* left Barra.

Like the *Admiral* the *Annie Jane* carried around 400 passengers, many of whom were Irish, from Armagh, Antrim and Cork. There were about a hundred Scottish emigrants, who were mostly young men, some with families, from Glasgow and the lowlands. They were skilled craftsmen, particularly carpenters, of the sort urgently needed in the rapidly expanding towns and cities of Canada. The rest of the below-deck passengers came from Lancashire. There were in addition a handful of cabin-class passengers, including Captain Rose and his wife. All of these people had paid their own fare including the cost of their provisions during the voyage, many already had jobs to go to in Canada, and all had sea chests with them packed with the most important of their personal possessions. And all were full of hope and expectation for the future. There was one final contrast between the passengers on the *Admiral* and those on the *Annie Jane*. Whereas almost all of the passengers on the *Admiral* had lived their entire lives on the Barra islands, three-quarters of those on the *Annie Jane*, though they did not know it yet, were to die there.

To the emigrants waiting to board her, the *Annie Jane* must have been a fine sight. The property of Thomas Holderness of Liverpool, she was brand new, having been built in Quebec and launched only three months earlier in May. Her maiden voyage from Quebec to England in June had been uneventful. The ship was a three-masted brig of oak and teak, and was approaching 200 feet long. She was built primarily to carry transatlantic emigrants and had

Emigrants destined for Quebec waiting to embark at Liverpool in 1852. (After *Illustrated London News*)

three decks as well as a capacious hold for cargo. She was rated A1 at Lloyds of London, and was captained by William Mason, a seaman with thirty-six years' experience at sea, including the captaincy of several other large ships. He commanded a crew of about forty, which included a surgeon, sailmaker, carpenter, first and second mates and two stewards. The deck hands were a mixture of British seamen and French-speaking Canadians.

The *Annie Jane* was due to sail on 19 August, but when passengers turned up with their sea chests at Sandon Dock that morning they were told they could not board yet as some of the cargo had been delayed. While they went off to find temporary accommodation, the loading of the *Annie Jane* continued. The bulk of her cargo was iron in one form or another, including about 400 tons of pig iron and iron bars. There was also a bulky iron boiler and 7-metre-long iron rails destined for the expanding rail network in Canada. Altogether, 800 tons of iron was put into the ships hold, along with 300 tons of general cargo including soap, tea, and ropes.

When the passengers were finally allowed on board, they found their berths were no different to those on the other ships carrying transatlantic emigrants at this time – cramped but just about adequate. Each passenger was allowed a notional 12 square feet of space, the equivalent of a 6-foot by 2-foot board, but with little more than 2-foot headspace between each level of bunks. They would occupy this space, with very little daylight, for the four or five weeks of the voyage. Altogether the ship could take about 400 below-deck passengers in these cramped conditions, and as the *Annie Jane* finally headed down the River Mersey on 24 August it had a full complement.

The ship headed northwards, passing the north-western tip of Ireland the next day before heading into the Atlantic. By midday on 25 August the wind had begun to freshen and gradually grew stronger over the next twenty-four hours. The *Annie Jane* began to reveal an uncomfortable propensity to pitch and roll which alarmed even some of the more experienced sailors on board. By late afternoon all hands were on deck along with Captain Mason, who ordered the 'royals' (the topmost sails) to be brought down. Shortly after a heavy wave hit the ship, she lurched violently, and the three top-masts and mizzenmast snapped and fell to the deck. Through the night the crew struggled to clear the debris as the ship continued to roll and pitch. Next day the sea and wind eased a little and the *Annie Jane* continued to sail westwards, but the passengers became increasingly frightened and were also voicing complaints about the lack of food and the overcrowded conditions. A group of them got together and presented a petition to the captain, setting out their grievances but, more importantly, urging him to turn the ship around and head back to Liverpool.

Captain Mason, First Mate Bell and Captain Rose went below to talk to the passengers and see for themselves conditions below deck after several days of heavy seas. What they heard and saw, together with their assessment of the damage suffered by the ship, led them to decide that the ship should indeed head back to Liverpool. Over the next four days as the winds continued to blow and shift, Captain Mason took the ship back down the west coast of Ireland, around Cape Clear, and then eastwards up St George's Channel to the mouth of the Mersey. On 31 August, after eight days and nearly 1,000 miles at sea, the passengers were finally able to set foot on firm ground again.

While repairs to the ship began immediately, the passengers put their complaints to the emigration officer at Liverpool, insisting that not every passenger had a berth, and some berths were 'double-booked'. In other words the ship had carried more passengers than were officially accounted for. They also complained that they had been given inadequate provisions and at times nothing to eat at all. They wanted their money back. The emigration officer and the ship's owner, Thomas Holderness, refused to agree to this, but three days later Holderness gave each of the petitioners 2/- by way of compensation.

By now repairs were nearing completion, and the bulk of the previous passengers were preparing to board the *Annie Jane* and to continue their journey to North America. Some passengers had decided that nothing would induce them to sail in the ship again, but there was no shortage of other would-be emigrants to take their place. Captain Rose and his wife resumed their occupation of a cabin, and they were joined in cabin class by four Swiss theologians and two other passengers. When the ship finally left port again on the evening of Thursday 8 September there were at least 385 below-deck passengers on board, though some were later to claim that there were considerably more than this.

The passage up the North Channel, past first the Isle of Man and then the northern tip of Ireland, was uneventful and calm. The *Annie Jane* headed north-westwards into the Atlantic, and it was not until the afternoon of Monday 12 September that a strong south-westerly wind strengthened and the ship began to pitch and roll. By night-time she was rolling badly and shortly before midnight the foreyard broke and damaged the bow of the ship so that she took in water. For two days while the strong south-westerly continued the crew were unable to clear the debris, while the ship moved slowly further into the North Atlantic.

By the time the south-westerly finally abated on Thursday 15 September, the passengers were highly alarmed at the state she was in, and that this voyage seemed to be following the pattern of the previous, unsuccessful, one. They apparently quietly sounded out the views of the first mate, Mr Bell, who in confidence told them he thought the ship would never make Quebec. So once more the passengers drew up a petition to the captain, urging him to return again to Liverpool and agreeing to forfeit their fares. It was said that all but half a dozen of the passengers signed it. When it was presented to Captain Mason his reaction was very different to that at the time of the previous petition. He tore it to shreds, tossed it into the wind, and said there would be no turning back. When the passengers remonstrated with him he pulled a pistol and said he was prepared to use it.

The passengers backed off, and for three days the ship continued on its north-westerly course. Nevertheless, Captain Mason realised that to continue the Atlantic crossing would be at best foolhardy, and at worst could prove fatal. With his limited options for hoisting an appropriate set of sails he was at the mercy of the winds. Finally, on Sunday 18 September with a north-westerly wind, he was able to set three sails and turn the *Annie Jane* around and set course for Ireland. But by late afternoon the wind had veered around to the south-west and Mason had to change course again. By Monday morning the south-westerly was blowing hard and another sail was lost; in the evening as the ship rolled badly the foreyard broke and went overboard.

For three days the ship was driven back north-westwards by the winds until on Thursday 22 September it was more than 200 miles north-west of St Kilda. Heavy seas continued to batter the ship and further damaged what remained of the riggings and masts. At last, on Saturday 24 September, as the wind dropped and veered round to blow from the north, Mason saw a chance to set some sort of sail and steer a course for Ireland. Using all his experience, ingenuity and seamanship, he got the crew to rig up something like a set of sails on what remained of the masts. The ship began to slowly head southwards. If the winds were kind and the weather held, the *Annie Jane* might reach the safety of Ireland in five or six days.

For four days the ship ploughed slowly southwards, and on the morning of the 28 September St Kilda came into view to the east and a few hours later the hills of the Western Isles were seen in the far distance. The sea was still calm, and there was sufficient wind to drive the ship along, and at 6.30 p.m. the lookouts spotted the Barra Head lighthouse standing at the edge of the 600-foot cliffs on the south coast of the tiny island of Berneray. At this point, the *Annie Jane* was passing the island of Sandray, and the nearest landfall on Ireland was 150 miles to the south. For a couple of hours the ship continued on its course. Among the crew and the passengers hopes were rising; but so, unexpectedly, was the wind. After five days of a favourable and gentle northerly, the wind suddenly veered around to blow from the south-west and within little more than an hour reached gale force. The ship was now entirely at the mercy of wind and wave.

Captain Mason asked Captain Rose for his opinion, and it seems they agreed that there was a real risk of being driven onto the bare rocks at the foot of the towering cliffs on the west coast of Mingulay. If the ship was wrecked there, then there was no hope for anyone. Mason made his decision – he would try to run the ship aground in the sandy bay on the west side of the island of Vatersay. The south-westerly was driving the ship towards the island, and Mason sent the crew to warn the passengers, and also to break down the bulkheads below deck to allow people to move as quickly and freely as possible when the time came.

The awesome cliffs of Berneray with the Barra Head lighthouse, which the crew of the *Annie Jane* sighted shortly before they were shipwrecked on Vatersay on 28 September 1853. (P. Foster)

Shortly before midnight the *Annie Jane* grounded near the southern tip of Bagh Siar (West Bay) on Vatersay. For a moment it seemed she had made a 'soft landing', but then she was suddenly hit by powerful waves which spun her around so that she was broadside onto the waves. Within minutes she began to break up. Accounts later given by survivors spoke of the tragic sights that followed. The second mate, Mr Markham, described how 'there would be about a hundred people on the poop ... and the fore part of the poop was washed away and the people with it'. Cabin passenger John Morgan said that a group of emigrants who had rushed on deck sought shelter in the cabins but that after the ship had been struck by the waves, they were all drowned. Taylor the steward, whose job it was to look after cabin-class passengers, described how Captain Rose and his wife were drowned when their cabin was swamped by a great wave. Other passengers, particularly women and children, hopefully sought shelter below deck but were inevitably drowned as the ship gradually broke apart.

The *Annie Jane* was torn into three pieces, with the bow still firmly stuck on the rocks at the entrance to the bay with a handful of the crew grimly clinging to what remained of it. The remains of the poop was further inshore and, by a miracle, nearly a hundred passengers and crew still clung to its ropes and tackle. Finally, the mid-section of the ship lay on its starboard side in shallow water near the beach, but here there were no survivors. After the wind had subsided around 2 a.m. those still clinging to the remains of the ship had to survive, cold and wet, until the sun came up and hopefully rescue might be at hand.

The morning of Sunday 29 September was bright and sunny with a calm sea and a light breeze. Bagh Siar, with its waters shading from deep blue to pale turquoise, its great white shell-sand beach, and its vivid green machair pasture, would have looked as beautiful as ever but for the horrific carnage which littered the beach and shallows. There were hundreds of broken fragments of timber from the shattered ship and remains of some of the ship's provisions and lighter items of cargo strewn across the beach. Scattered among this debris, and floating in the shallows, were the bodies of many of her passengers. Most were naked and many were badly battered, sometimes missing arms or legs.

About 7 a.m. some of the local farm labourers emerged from their blackhouses set back in the machair, and came down to the beach. Survivors clinging to the poop yelled and waved to their would-be rescuers. The Vatersay men waded cautiously out towards the wreck of the poop while a member of the *Annie Jane*'s crew with a rope tied around his waist plunged into the water and swam towards the beach. He soon reached the nearest of the Vatersay men and together they waded ashore and secured the rope. Meanwhile other survivors on the poop managed to manoeuvre what remained of the mizzenmast into a position where, with the aid of the rope, people were able to edge along the broken timber until they could drop into shallow water and wade ashore.

Captain Mason was the last to leave the remains of his ship, and when he finally managed a roll call of the survivors he found that they numbered 101. These included thirty-seven of the crew, sixty of the emigrants, and four of the cabin-class passengers. This meant that at least 333 had died in the tragedy – more if there were in fact a number of additional, unregistered passengers. The survivors were obviously cold, wet and weak and needed food and shelter, but both were in short supply on Vatersay. There were only eight households on the whole island, which was a single farm of which the tenant was Donald Maclellan, a native of the small island of Taransay near the Isle of Harris. He lived in the estate house previously occupied by the Macneils of Vatersay, which overlooked Bagh Siar. His labourers lived in blackhouses on the edge of the machair, and the 'farmyard' with its byres and barns was enclosed nearby.

Thirty of the survivors, including Captain Mason, senior crew members and the cabin-class passengers, were taken up to the estate house and somehow accommodated in this modest building. The rest of the survivors were taken into the blackhouses, barns and byres. The population of Vatersay had risen overnight from sixty-four (of which twenty were children) to 165. Most of these people lived at subsistence level and would have little food to spare. In the circumstances it is hardly surprising that many of the survivors later complained of getting little to eat while they were on the island. The first survivors eventually left the island for Mull about a week after the disaster, the rest following soon after. Captain Mason sent a letter to Thomas Holderness with the first evacuees, in which he said that about 200 bodies had been washed ashore. They had been interred in pits dug close to the shore.

An enquiry into the disaster was duly opened in Liverpool on 1 November 1853 and submitted its report on 30 December. It concluded that there were a number of factors that contributed to the tragedy, including badly stowed cargo and the inadequacies of the French-Canadian crew members. There was some evidence to support both these allegations, and several survivors had mentioned the problems that had arisen with the French-Canadians, but one wonders if they were to some extent used as scapegoats. The problems with the stowage of cargo, and particularly of course with the pig iron and iron rails, seem more important. After the first abandoned voyage the cargo had been unloaded and stowed differently, suggesting that Captain Mason perhaps thought that the cargo had affected the ship's behaviour. One experienced cross-Atlantic traveller who had seen it was reported as saying that 'her damned cargo will sink her to the bottom'. One of the most notable and repeated comments made by survivors of both voyages was how the *Annie Jane* rolled so badly even in relatively low seas. The way the cargo was stowed may have been crucial, because it was the excessive rolling of the ship which seemed to be responsible for the repeated and crucial loss of masts and sails.

If the cargo was to blame, then presumably the re-stowing of it had still not resolved the problem, for the fact is that the *Annie Jane* seems to have behaved just as badly on the second voyage as she did on the first. By the time Mason finally turned her around and began the slow journey back towards Ireland she was already seriously damaged. It was then the ship's misfortune to run into one of the worst equinoctial storms that Britain had witnessed for many years. On the same night that the *Annie Jane* went down, ships all round the coasts of Britain were running into problems and other smaller ships were driven ashore or wrecked. But none suffered the huge loss of life of the *Annie Jane*.

Sometime around 1880 a private individual commissioned a memorial to those who perished on the *Annie Jane*. It was erected on the dunes behind the beach, where it still stands today. The inscription on it reads:

> On September 28th 1853 the ship 'Annie Jane' with emigrants from Liverpool to Quebec was totally wrecked in this bay and three-fourths of the crew and passengers numbering about 350 men, women, and children were drowned and their bodies interred here.

And there they remain to this day – or do they? The first Ordnance Survey map of Vatersay published in 1878 (before the memorial was erected) has the inscription 'Graves of 280 shipwrecked emigrants' written along the north side of the bay and curving around onto the north end of the dunes behind the beach. As the memorial stands towards the southern end of the area marked by the inscription, it might be assumed that the OS map maker meant that the burial place was at the point where the inscription ends. But an earlier map, surveyed less than ten years after the disaster, has exactly the same inscription attached to a divided rectangle placed very clearly above the north shore of the bay. It appears to be a fenced enclosure. The location is quite precise, and so too is the number of dead – no suggestion of rounding up to 300 or 350. So do we assume that the person who erected the memorial had the OS map and simply assumed that the end of the inscription marked the burial place, while in fact the victims were buried about 400 metres away?

Possibly, but this solution to the problem is itself problematical for two reasons. Firstly it is quite a difficult spot to reach and would have involved the handful of people available to carry out the burials carrying 280 decomposing bodies a considerable distance and up over a difficult rocky shoreline to reach the supposed burial place. Secondly, having reached this spot it would have been impossible to dig any sort of 'pit' big enough and deep enough to take nearly 300 bodies because the soil on this slope just east of the blackhouses at Tresivick is very shallow. It must have been easier and quicker to dig pits into

The monument to the victims of the *Annie Jane* set up on the dunes beneath which they are allegedly buried.

the dunes behind the beach where the bodies were recovered. Certainly when we surveyed this stretch of coastline in the 1990s we noted no trace of an old enclosure which might have been that marked on the nineteenth-century map. There is no resolution to this problem. We could perhaps suppose that a small number of victims were indeed buried separately on the slopes near Tresivick for reasons which we could only speculate about, and the rest placed in the pits in the dunes. Wherever their mortal remains lie, the victims from the *Annie Jane* surely deserve to rest in peace.

12

The Vatersay Raiders – The Cottars Revolt 1900–1910

For a few days in 1853 the news of the *Annie Jane* disaster propelled Vatersay into the national news, though as many of the newspaper reports unconsciously revealed, people knew little or nothing about Vatersay and most of what they did know was garbled. But in 1906 Vatersay was once more in the news and a topic of heated debate in government, among the landed classes, and among those who were concerned about the future of the highlands and islands. The case of the Vatersay Raiders caused a political storm.

The roots of the situation which threw up the raiders was one that we have already touched on in several of the preceding chapters in this book. Since the late eighteenth century Barra and its islands had been overcrowded. As the population grew, new crofts were laid out on inferior land, particularly around the coasts, and some crofts were divided to create more – but less sustainable – tenancies. The increasing creation of farms saw significant numbers of crofts eliminated altogether. The inevitable result was that many crofters lived increasingly impoverished lives made worse by having no security of tenure and being at the mercy of variations in the weather. At the same time the shortage of even unsatisfactory crofts and the growing population saw an ever growing number of landless 'cottars' who eked out an existence only through the kindness of relatives and friends who shared with them what few resources they had. The scale of the problem can be gauged by the numbers of cottars found in some of the Barra townships in 1883. In Kentangaval there were twenty crofting households, but twenty-four cottar families. In Castlebay cottar families outnumbered crofters by thirty to twenty-two, and in Earsary fourteen cottar families squatted alongside twenty-two crofters.

The problem was by no means unique to Barra, and it led to various confrontations between crofters and cottars on the one hand and the landlords, factors and police on the other. On Skye in 1882 the clash between 500 protesters and the landlord's men supported by fifty Glasgow policemen came to be dubbed 'the Battle of The Braes', and led to marines being stationed

Castlebay schoolhouse, where the Crofting Commission met on 26 May 1883.

on Skye until 1885. The government intervened in 1883 by establishing a Crofting Commission 'to inquire into the conditions of the crofters and cottars in the highlands and islands'. Headed by Lord Napier and Ettrick, the members of the Commission undertook an extensive tour and held more than sixty meetings to hear and see at first hand the problems facing the crofters and cottars.

On 26 May 1883 they came to Barra and took over Castlebay schoolhouse to hear the evidence of six crofters and cottars and that of the factor for the whole estate, Ranald Macdonald, and of Dr M'Gillivray, the tenant of the Eoligarry farm which now held about a third of the land on Barra. The principal witness for the crofters was Michael Buchanan of Borve, who lived on his brother's croft. He told Lord Napier that the crofters' main complaints were that their plots were too small to be viable, that the quality of the land left much to be desired, and that the landlord's factor and officers treated the tenants harshly. He was at pains to say, however, that 'the inhabitants of this island have every confidence in their present proprietrix'.

That proprietrix was Lady Emily Gordon Cathcart (hereafter Lady Cathcart). By one of those curious little quirks of fate that history throws up, Emily had been born in 1845 in Madras, where her father was in the Civil Service. At that time, the last ancestral owner of Barra, General Macneil was commanding a regiment in Poona, and in 1848, when Emily was three years old, he moved to take up a command in Madras. But Emily and her family had moved back to Britain in 1847, so they were never to meet. The General held the ownership of Barra for fourteen years; Emily held it for fifty-two, until her

Lady Emily Gordon Cathcart, daughter-in-law of Colonel Gordon of Cluny, who inherited the estate of Barra in 1878 and had to face the problem of the Vatersay Raiders. (Courtesy of Robert Lindzee Gordon)

death in 1932. Emily had inherited the estate when her first husband, John Gordon, died in 1878. He in turn had inherited it from his father, Colonel Gordon of Cluny, the notorious clearer of Barra.

The outcome of the Crofting Commission was the Crofters Holdings (Scotland) Act of 1886 which went some way to resolve the worst of the problems facing the crofters. It gave them security of tenure, guaranteed them compensation for any improvements they made to their croft, and set up measures to fix fair rents. Although there were still unresolved problems, crofters throughout the highlands and islands welcomed the Act with open arms. But despite the Commission's remit to look into the conditions of 'the crofters and cottars', the Crofters Act, as perhaps its name implies, did little or nothing to help the landless cottars. In the celebrations which greeted the Act in 1886, they were the forgotten people.

With the setting up of the Congested Districts Board (hereafter CDB) in 1897 hopes were raised that the problem might be resolved, but with no powers of compulsory purchase the Board's scope for decisive action in creating more crofts was limited. On Barra tensions boiled over in September 1900 and cottars from the eastern townships raided the farm at Northbay. Within days, forty cottars from the south of the island had crossed to Vatersay, where they measured and marked out twenty-one notional crofts. They then sent a letter to Lady Cathcart asking for crofts on the island and openly threatening to seize the land if the crofts were not granted. Ranald MacDonald, Lady Cathcart's secretary – a man well known since the time of the crofting commission as unsympathetic to both crofters and cottars – turned the application down flat. This sparked off further raids in October and the following February when more notional crofts were marked out at Caolis and Uidh at the north end of Vatersay.

At this point, however, the CDB managed to negotiate the purchase of 3,000 acres of the Eoligarry estate and established fifty-eight new crofts on the land around Northbay. While this did much for the cottars at the north end of Barra, it only increased the unrest among those in the townships around Castlebay. In 1901 there were over 2,400 inhabitants of Barra, including hundreds of cottars and their dependents. From Castlebay they could gaze across the water at the island of Vatersay rented out as a farm by Donald Macdonald. On Vatersay little more than a dozen permanent inhabitants were surrounded by excellent pastures and some patches of reasonable arable land. No wonder that cottars cast envious eyes on this green and pleasant land just a twenty-minute boat ride away.

Inevitably further raids followed in 1901 and 1902, to which the forces of law and order, and the government, turned a blind eye. However, in 1903 the CDB, gallantly trying to help within the limits of what it could do, purchased 60 acres of land at Uidh specifically for cottars from Barra to grow potatoes. But this only whetted the appetite of the cottars and more raids followed in

1904 and 1905. These sporadic raids might have continued for years, but by now the cottars had acquired an unelected but forceful leader in Duncan Campbell of Kentangaval. In 1905 he sent another letter to Lady Cathcart on behalf of sixty-two cottars asking that when the lease on Vatersay farm ran out, it should be divided into crofts. By the end of the year he had still received no reply, so in December he wrote to Donald MacDonald, the tenant farmer, telling him plainly that the cottars intended to take over the whole island.

The following February forty-three cottars landed on Vatersay and, led by a lone piper, marched to the farmyard below the estate house. Here they marked out fourteen crofts, spent an hour celebrating their success and then returned to Castlebay. But within days two more raids had taken place, the second seeing the laying out of forty more crofts near the estate house. These symbolic actions were followed in mid-June by the shipping of cattle from Barra to Vatersay. Lady Cathcart's solicitors appealed to the government to take action but the government washed its hands of the matter. Duncan Campbell sensed it was now an opportune time to take the raids onto a new level. At the end of July forty cottars invaded Vatersay, selected croft sites near the estate house and began to repair the farmyard walls with the intention of creating temporary roofed dwellings there.

Donald MacDonald who had watched all this from his estate house with some fear and trepidation and had waited in vain for the police to uphold the law eventually decided he had to take action. He rounded up all the cattle and horses that had been brought over by the raiders, penned them up, and sent the cottars a message that if they wanted their animals back they would have to pay for their release. The cottars, led by Duncan Campbell, soon confronted MacDonald and demanded the animals' release. When he refused, they simply opened the pens and let the animals out themselves. The situation soon developed into farce, with MacDonald getting his men to ferry animals back to Barra in the morning and the cottars bringing them back again in the afternoon.

Now Campbell raised the stakes yet again, by encouraging the cottars to start building huts on the plots they had marked out. He demolished his own hut at Kentangaval and moved it to Vatersay, where by Christmas 1906 three huts had been completed. By the spring of 1907 the number of huts had risen to thirteen and the cottar settlement was taking on the appearance of something permanent. Lady Cathcart, despairing of the government or the police protecting her property, initiated legal proceedings in April 1907. Injunctions were served on eleven of the raiders, five of whom proved not to come from Barra but from Mingulay.

The island of Mingulay, little more than 5 miles south of Vatersay, was populated by about 130 people at this time. It did not have the same resources of pasture or arable plots that Vatersay had, even though it boasted some of the finest and highest cliffs in the British Isles. The sea crossing to it could be

Vatersay township with modern houses occupying the sites where the raiders built their huts in 1907. The ruins of the farmhouse from which Donald Macdonald looked down on the invasion of his farm can be seen bottom right.

treacherous and there was no decent harbour or landing place. Its inhabitants were growing increasingly restless and a few had already left the island before 1907. Now, they sensed a heaven-sent opportunity to escape to somewhere better.

Following Lady Cathcart's injunctions, the Sheriff of Invernesshire visited Vatersay and talked at length to several of the raiders, concluding that they were 'respectable men – most anxious to do as little harm as possible to the tenant of the farm'. The government, feeling they had to do something, suggested to Lady Cathcart that she should create crofts on the island with financial and other assistance from the CDB.

Lady Cathcart refused the invitation for a number of reasons and told the government bluntly that they should either purchase the island or get on and do their duty to uphold the law. Meanwhile, further huts were being erected by raiding cottars and by February 1908 over thirty cottars had settled on Vatersay, and two Mingulay families had built huts on the empty neighbouring island of Sandray.

Having seen no improvement in the situation since the injunctions were served eight months previously, in January 1908 Lady Cathcart pursued the eleven cottars originally served with the injunctions for breach of interdict and contempt of court. Now the Vatersay Raiders were about to be catapulted into national fame. On 2 June 1908 ten raiders (one had escaped the net by oversight) stood before the Court of Sessions in Edinburgh, dressed for the occasion in their traditional fishing garb. They listened while counsel for Lady Cathcart briefly set out the case against them. Their own counsel began by admitting that the men were guilty on both counts but he claimed they had really been given little choice by the dire circumstances in which they and their families had found themselves. Lord Justice Clerk dismissed the men's explanation for their actions as immaterial and sentenced each man to two months' imprisonment. To the sentence he added a stark warning that should they repeat the raids after their release, then the law would be applied less leniently next time.

By mid-afternoon the ten were on their way to jail – in taxis hired by their agent to avoid the indignity of the prison van. Within days petitions for their release were being organised all over Scotland, the *Edinburgh Evening News* opened a relief fund for the families of the incarcerated men, and the media began to take the government to task for its lack of action and its failure to agree terms with Lady Cathcart. They were finally forced into serious negotiations with Lady Cathcart, and on 18 July terms were agreed and Lady Cathcart immediately petitioned for the release of the prisoners. The men emerged after six weeks in prison, still in their fishing garb, and were soon on the train to Oban. They arrived back in Castlebay on board the steamer *Lapwing* to a heroes' welcome from a huge crowd.

With 200 'illegal' inhabitants now on Vatersay, it was obviously desirable that the crofts should be laid out and allocated as soon as possible. But the final terms were yet to be agreed between Lady Cathcart and the CDB since they were still arguing about the compensation that Lady Cathcart would get for the fall in the rental income from Vatersay from £330 p.a. as a farm, to £180 p.a. given over to crofts. Eventually the government had no choice – they decided they had to buy the island from Lady Cathcart. After further wrangling over the price, Lady Cathcart finally wrote to the Board on 30 November 1908 agreeing to accept £6,250 for Vatersay.

She also sold them the island of Sandray which was to be used as common grazing for the southern townships of Eorisdale and Vatersay. It was not until April 1909 that the CDB was finally able to invite applications to take up the sixty crofts they intended to create on the island.

When the application process closed, they had received eighty-two applications for sixty crofts. The CDB now had the delicate task of deciding which applications would be successful – one in four would be disappointed. It was assumed that preference would be given to those who had already occupied land on Vatersay, those whose ancestors had originally been evicted from the island in the early nineteenth century, and to landless cottars. But the board took account of other criteria too – were the men of good character, what experience and skills did they have, and what resources? When the names of the successful applicants were announced many of the original raiders had not been awarded a croft, including three of those who had spent six weeks in Edinburgh

The Vatersay Raiders, dressed in borrowed suits, photographed before they attended their trial on 2 June 1908. (Comunn Eachdraidh Bharraigh agus Bhatarsaigh)

The Mingulay families who raided Sandray, outside their houses at Sheader. (Dom Odo Blundell)

jail. Needless to say there was a general sense of outrage and a great deal of
anger – and anguish – among the raiders who had been excluded. Over the
next two years some of the unfortunate applicants were awarded crofts which
others had not taken up and some moved to Barra.

Meanwhile the handful of crofters still occupying Mingulay were threatened
with eviction in 1911 when Lady Cathcart decided to rent out the island with
its smaller neighbours Berneray and Pabbay to Jonathan Maclean of Barra.
Places were found for them elsewhere and the last inhabitant left Mingulay in
the summer of 1912. As to the raiders who had occupied Sandray, they had
applied for crofts to be established on Sandray but their request was rejected
and they too were moved on, most of them eventually settling on Vatersay.
The last of the Sandray Raiders left Sheader in March 1911.

Although these events happened only a century ago there is little trace of
the original raiders' houses. Many were temporary wooden structures which
have long since been pulled down and replaced by new houses. But if one
should ever get to Sandray, one can step back a hundred years and enter the
five houses built at Sheader by the raiders from Mingulay. Unusually they
were built as a continuous 'terrace', as if their occupants wanted to make a
statement about their unity and solidarity. We recorded the site in 1991 and
noted a long sequence of occupation which subsequent excavation showed to
begin in the Bronze Age. Iron Age and medieval occupation was followed by
at least four phases of post-medieval settlement, the last of which was that of
the raiders. The raiders' houses were substantial buildings, given they were
erected quickly and with no certainty of prolonged occupation. Each had
a well-built fireplace and chimney in its west wall and a door in its north-
facing wall. Excavations in the house which we believe was occupied by John
Macneil revealed a floor of trampled soil, across which a 'path' of stone slabs
led from the door to the back wall. Four large stone slabs set in line across the

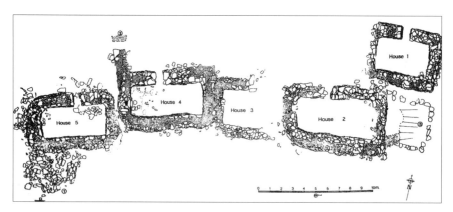

The 'terrace' of blackhouses built at Sheader by the Sandray Raiders from Mingulay.
(P. Foster)

The excavation of house 4 at Sheader with its fireplace in the west wall, and the lined hearth of an underlying house revealed beneath the earth floor. (P. Foster)

width of the building were the base for a wooden partition, which created a room about 3 metres by 2 metres at the east end of the house. The remaining space was undivided. In other words although this building was not erected until 1908, it was essentially a blackhouse with no windows in its walls, but the central hearth had been replaced by a fireplace and chimney built into an end wall. The other houses all appeared the same, and they were therefore rather different to the timber houses which most of the raiders from Barra constructed.

For a brief period the Vatersay Raiders caught the attention of the people of Scotland in a way which none of the other land raids in the highlands and islands did. Those on Barra and Vatersay descended from the raiders still recall their activities with pride. They have earned themselves a permanent niche in the history not only of Barra but of the highlands and islands as a whole. As for Lady Gordon Cathcart, she continued as the owner of the estate of Barra until her death in 1932. After lengthy negotiations it was purchased in 1937 by Robert Lister Macneil, a descendent of Hector Ban Macneil, tacksman of Earsary, who took 370 Barra emigrants to Nova Scotia in 1802. In 1915 he had been recognised by the Court of the Lord Lyon as the Macneil of Barra, so that a hundred years after the General had lost the ancestral estate it was back in Macneil hands. In 2004 his son, Ian Roderick Macneil, forty-sixth chief of the Macneils, gave the crofting estate to the Scottish nation.

Further Reading

I provide suggestions here for further reading only about sites and episodes on Barra and its islands.

For an overview of the archaeology of Barra and its neighbouring islands:
K. Branigan and P. Foster, *Barra and the Bishop Isles* (Tempus 2002).

For a guide to the sites and monuments:
K. Branigan, *Ancient Barra* (Comhairle nan Eilean Siar 2007).

For a collection of folklore and oral traditions about the history of Barra:
J. MacPherson, *Tales from Barra Told by the Coddy* (Birlinn 1992).

Pioneers: The excavations at Allt Easdal are published in K. Branigan and P. Foster, *Barra. Archaeological Research on Ben Tangaval* (Sheffield Academic Press 1995).

Mourners: The 'giant cists' of Bretadale are published in Branigan and Foster 1995 (above). Standing stones and stone rings, Bronze Age cairns, and the excavations of kerbed cairns are all described in K. Branigan and P. Foster, *From Barra to Berneray* (Sheffield Academic Press 2000).

Tower Builders: The brochs on Barra and nearby islands and the excavations at Dun Ruadh on Pabbay are described in Branigan and Foster 2000 (above). The excavation of the wheelhouse at Allt Easdal is described in the same volume. The wheelhouse in Allasdale was published by A. Young in *Proceedings of the Society of Antiquaries of Scotland* 89 (1955), 290–328.

Norsemen: The excavations of the Norse shielings at Allt Easdal and Ben Gunnary are reported in Branigan and Foster 2000 above. A discussion of

Norse place names in Barra by C. Borgstrom was published in *The Book of Barra* ed. J. L. Campbell (paperback edition Acair 1998). A summary of the Norse houses excavated in South Uist can be found in M. Parker-Pearson, N. Sharples and J. Symonds, *South Uist* (Tempus 2004).

Outlaws: A colourful account of the early Macneils of Barra can be found in R. L. Macneil, *The Clan Macneil* (Scotpress 1985), and the same author describes the renovation and discusses the history of Kisimul Castle in *The Castle in the Sea* (Collins 1964). The wreck of the *Adelaar* and its twentieth century excavation are described by C. Martin in the *International Journal of Nautical Archaeology* 34.2 (2005), 178–210.

Jacobites: The information about the Macneil's involvement in the Jacobite rebellion of 1745 was brought together by J. L. Campbell in an article in the *Innes Review* 17 (1966), most easily available in J. L. Campbell, *A Very Civil People* (Birlinn 2000).

Gentleman Farmer: Much of the evidence for Roderick the Gentle's chiefdom is brought together in K. Branigan, *From Clan to Clearance* (Oxbow 2005). His letters are published in J. L. Campbell, *The Book of Barra* (paperback edition, Acair 1998).

Emigrants: The documentary evidence for emigrations from Barra is brought together in K. Branigan 2005 (above), which also includes a detailed catalogue of known emigrants. Some of the episodes are discussed at length in J. Bumsted, *The People's Clearance* (1982).

The General: The life of General Roderick Macneil is the subject of K. Branigan, *The Last of the Clan* (Amberley 2010).

The Entrepreneur: Gordon of Cluny's involvement with Barra is discussed in detail in K. Branigan 2005 (above), which also publishes the excavations at Balnbodach. There is more about Gordon in E. Richards, *The Highland Clearances* (Birlinn 2000).

Lost Souls: A good account of the tragedy, bringing together reports from the newspapers of the time and a summary of the evidence given at the enquiry was published by Bob Charnley, *Shipwrecked on Vatersay* (Maclean Press 1992)

The Vatersay Raiders: Ben Buxton's excellent book *The Vatersay Raiders* (Birlinn 2008) brings all the evidence together. His *Mingulay. An Island and its People* (Birlinn 1995) also has much of relevance to the Raiders. Excavations at Sheader are published in K. Branigan 2005 (above).

Acknowledgements

Over the period of more than twenty years that I have been researching the archaeology and history of Barra and its neighbouring islands I have received help, information, advice and encouragement from dozens of people, not only on Barra and in the British Isles, but also in Canada, the USA, and Italy. I am pleased to have the opportunity to say a collective thank you to them all. Special mention must be made of my colleagues who made working on the islands not only academically rewarding but also a pleasure and, to be honest, a great deal of fun – Patrick Foster, David Gilbertson, and Colin Merrony. I also owe much to our project officer, Angie Foster, and to the several hundred students who played a vital part in our work and again were a pleasure to work with.

Our work was only possible due to the permission to work on the islands willingly given by Ian Macneil, the Department of Agriculture & Fisheries, and the Barra Head Sheepstock Co. Equally we relied entirely on the goodwill of the crofters and their grazing committees, and on the seamanship of John Allen Macneil and Calum Macneil to get us to the more remote islands. To all of them I am very grateful.

I am pleased also to have the opportunity to thank all those institutions which provided the vital financial support for our work. There would have been no project but for an initial grant from the Robert Kiln Trust, and the University of Sheffield provided support each year of the project. Other significant support was awarded by the British Academy. The biggest share of the costs was borne by Historic Scotland, and I am grateful not only to them for their grants but for the sound support and advice we got from Patrick Ashmore, Olwyn Owen and Noel Fojut.

In preparing this book for publication I am particularly indebted to Holly Branigan and Stuart Boutell, who sorted out endless IT and photographic problems, a fair proportion of them caused by my own ineptitude. As always I have relied on Nong to read the text and correct lapses in my spelling and grammar, and even more so for moral support and encouragement when the going got tough.

Most of the pictures in this book are from my own collection, but I have to thank the following individuals for generously providing illustrations: David Brinn, Stuart Boutell, Ian Fletcher, Patrick Foster, Robert Lindzee Gordon, Colin Martin, Niall Sharples, David Savary and Geoff Watts. I am also particularly grateful to the following for permission to reproduce pictures in their collections: National Galleries of Scotland, Comunn Eachdraidh Bharraigh agus Bhatarsaigh, Public Archives of Nova Scotia, Public Archives of Prince Edward Island, Musée de Versailles, National Archives of Scotland, Royal Commission for Ancient & Historical Monuments of Scotland, Museum of the Queen's Own Highlanders and the Architect of the Capitol USA.

Index